THE
ENFORCER
A LIFE FIGHTING CRIME

THE
ENFORCER
A LIFE FIGHTING CRIME

GRAEME PEARSON
with Kevin O'Hare

BLACK & WHITE PUBLISHING

First published 2008
by Black & White Publishing Ltd
29 Ocean Drive, Edinburgh EH6 6JL

1 3 5 7 9 10 8 6 4 2 08 09 10 11 12

ISBN: 978 1 84502 215 0

A CIP catalogue record for this book is available from
The British Library.

Typeset by Ellipsis Books Limited, Glasgow
Printed and bound by MPG Books Ltd, Bodmin

TO MY MOTHER AND FATHER

Contents

Foreword

In thirty-eight years' service as a police officer, I enjoyed a privileged insight into the lives of thousands of people. I saw the best and worst that people could do to one another while attempting to resolve differences and solve crimes.

I closed my police career as Director General of the Scottish Crime and Drug Enforcement Agency, which gave me the opportunity to tackle criminals who seek to control organised crime in our country. This job provided my biggest challenges and also some of the darkest moments of my career.

This book is a frank account of the highs and lows of my experiences. I hope that it will inspire youngsters to become police officers and others to wonder whether they should perhaps have joined the service.

I have mentioned only a few police officers by name and this is to protect the privacy of others. However, I am happy to acknowledge that I would have achieved very little without the men and women who taught and worked alongside me. I look back on my police career with immense fondness and gratitude.

I shared the worst moments affecting many ordinary people, often in dreadful circumstances. Sometimes, even prisoners trusted me with their biggest secrets and disappointments. My recollections may surprise you but I also hope that they comfort you.

During my years in the service, I met a number of evil men and convicted them against the odds. Nevertheless, I am convinced that the majority of those in prison are not evil by nature but lack the ability to cope with the pressures of modern day life. I have learned that we need to ensure that those who seek to profit from criminality are stripped of all their assets; this would ensure they could no longer be role models. We need to take steps to keep our young people away from a life of crime.

Everything in this book really happened to me. I make no apologies for my views or the way they are reported. Others may have different recollections, but I am sure they will forgive me as I am confident the essential details are beyond challenge.

Graeme Pearson
Glasgow, 2008

1
Getting to Grips
with a Triple Killer

It was a typically miserable cold and wet February night back in 1980 and at times like these the night shift could be pretty challenging. The previous day, blizzards had left Scotland cut off but at least the night had now turned crisp and dry. As usual, I left my house not knowing what would happen in the next few hours but for me that was always one of the really great things about being a police officer.

That night, as I'd often done before, I left home a little early to visit an informant before my shift started. Informants, or touts as they are known in Glasgow parlance, were hard to develop so it was essential to spend time keeping them onside. I often met touts at their homes, a trick I had picked up from older detectives, but I'd always park a fair distance away just to make sure I wasn't seen. I would then cut through the backcourts to make sure no one was following me.

These visits gave me the opportunity to develop a real bond with an informant and also showed the tout how we could work together. Touts in my experience felt far more relaxed in their own environment. They also opened up more easily when it came to talking business. Often on such visits I would glean some valuable information about an ongoing crime or be told something that was about to happen.

On this terrible night, I remember being greeted as usual

like an old friend and given a cup of tea and some toast as we sat down to discuss the Glasgow criminal underworld. Our conversation was suddenly halted by the headlines on the nine o'clock news. Three people had been viciously murdered at Gartnavel Hospital in Glasgow. We both sat in silence, hanging on every word of the awful news.

The news report said that around 5pm that evening Joyce Harkins, a 25-year-old clerical assistant at Gartnavel Hospital, having picked up her four-year-old son, James, from the hospital crèche, had then met up with her brother, Peter Flynn, before heading home after her day's work. Then, outside the hospital, a man came up to Joyce and, within minutes, the three of them had been viciously stabbed to death for no apparent reason.

Even by Glasgow's standards, these murders were extreme – in a matter of moments three lives had been needlessly and senselessly taken.

As the news report finished, the tout said, 'You'll be looking for her husband or "man".' As I nodded in agreement, it was one of many times that I realised how alike some criminals and police think. We have a special understanding of life that comes from getting under the skin and being so close to criminality. Little did I know, just a few hours later, how close up and personal I would get to this triple killer.

By 11pm, I was on duty as the night shift detective sergeant at Temple police office, then the headquarters of the Serious Crime Squad. Gartnavel Hospital was barely a mile away from the office but, at the handover from the late shift, we were all told that the division's detectives were out in Thornliebank following a definite line of enquiry. So, I presumed the killer would soon be in custody.

The four of us on duty that night split up into two groups as we left the office. Along with a fellow detective – or 'neighbour' as we officers call our partners – I was soon driving towards the city centre when an urgent message on the police car radio told us to head for the tiny Thornliebank police sub-office as quickly as possible. I thought I was probably needed to take a voluntary statement from the murder accused, something which, at that time in my career, I had done on a number of occasions.

As I pulled up outside the tiny police office, it was obvious something was seriously amiss. Firearms officers were dashing around the street and the bosses were deep in a meeting which I was invited to join. In the room were the two officers running the triple murder enquiry, Detective Superintendent Alex Michie and Detective Chief Inspector Charlie Craig, both deep in conversation. I knew them well as I had worked for them in various police offices across the city.

They told an unbelievably bizarre and horrific tale. John Harkins, Joyce's estranged husband, had turned up at the home of one of his former work colleagues. Harkins then told this man that he had killed his own wife, son and brother-in-law. At first, the family did not believe him but they could tell something was seriously wrong by his demeanour. They only believed him when they heard the television news reporting the triple killing at Gartnavel Hospital.

Harkins' colleague, Raymond Murray, didn't know what to do but left the house on the pretext of buying a carry-out and promised to return with it as quickly as possible. Once outside the house, Raymond had met a friend, Frank McIlree, who urged him to get in touch with the police as quickly as possible.

So, by the time I arrived in Thornliebank, Harkins, a mortuary technician, was in Raymond Murray's home in nearby Locheil Road with Murray's wife and three children. Harkins was obviously unstable, so we had no way of gauging how he would respond when the police turned up.

By now it was after midnight and the house was surrounded with armed officers, although no one had yet made an attempt to contact or approach the killer or the wife inside. By now, Raymond Murray was understandably very agitated and struggling to cope with the pressure. He was beside himself with worry about what could be happening inside his home.

Raymond barely knew Harkins, whom he had worked alongside as a mortuary assistant at the Royal Infirmary. From his work, Raymond was only too aware of the terrible impact violence had in Glasgow and he was terrified for his family left inside a house with a man who that very afternoon had so viciously slashed three innocent people to death.

It was getting late and it was time for some action but a plan of sorts had been worked out. Raymond was going to return to the house with his carry-out and two friends he had met in the pub. Once inside the house, the friends were going to pounce on the suspect and overcome him, allowing the undercover officers outside enough time to enter and arrest him. It didn't seem much of a plan but by now it had been three hours since Raymond had walked out of his home.

Our bosses needed a long-haired friend who didn't look like a police officer and that was why they had sent for me. Frank McIlree, a small, gallus, powerfully built man was also keen to help in any way possible.

Ten minutes later, Raymond, my new friend Frank and I were heading along the street to the house. It was a typical four-in-a-block council house with a front door leading to a staircase and all the rooms on the upper storey. As we walked towards it, I explained to the others how important it was to try to behave as normally as possible so we could get as near to Harkins as possible. We needed to walk up the stairs slowly, so as not to spook him. There were far too many stairs for us to be able to surprise Harkins. The plan was that as soon as we were near enough, Frank and I would overcome him, using as much violence as was necessary to protect the others in the house. I had my detective's stave and Frank had the carry-out. How could we fail?

As we approached the enclosed garden in Locheil Road, I exchanged a nervous smile with the firearms officer hidden in the hedgerow. He had been startled by our sudden appearance and I made it clear that I didn't want him to shoot any of us when he entered the house in the next few minutes. He looked at me as if I was insane as I headed into the house after all this time, pretending nothing was amiss. I was thinking something similar but it was difficult to see any other way to end the stand-off. For all we knew, Harkins might have already killed everyone in the house, or even worse, might kill them if the police made a wrong approach by opening negotiations.

As we reached the stairwell, Harkins was already standing at the top of the stairs looking extremely anxious. He was a slim, sinewy man who already appeared suspicious at our arrival. He asked Raymond what had kept him. True to his script, Raymond introduced me and Frank as his pals from the pub and then produced the carry-out. We chatted as the three of us headed up the stairs and by the time we got to the top landing Harkins had retreated to the living room.

Frank and I stepped forward and, once we were within striking distance, I pulled out my police baton from under my coat and Frank produced a Glasgow surprise – he had hidden a small hammer in his polythene bag and suddenly produced it from the carry-out.

Seconds later, Harkins was laid out on the floor with the two of us on top of him after we had hit him several times around the head. Almost immediately, three or four police officers arrived, Harkins was in custody and the siege was over. To everyone's relief, Raymond's wife and children were all safe.

During the melee, Frank and I had been hit on the back of our heads by police batons but were uninjured. I'm sure

Frank was quicker off the mark than me and had laid the first blow on Harkins. He had a done a superb job and, like me, was so relieved that it was all over.

Within minutes, I found myself back out on the street milling about with uniformed and detective colleagues, slightly shaken by the speed of events. In a matter of minutes we had arrested a man capable of killing three decent human beings and without ceremony he had been whisked away to custody.

In the quiet of the night it was hard to comprehend the sheer relief felt by the Murray family. They knew how close they had come to tragedy, through no fault of their own, and to the evil that Harkins was clearly capable of. At the same time it occurred to me that but for the willingness of ordinary people like Frank McIlree, our communities could be a less attractive prospect.

As for the police intervention, there was some friendly teasing the following day thanks to the fact that a serious crime squad officer had been struck on the head by one of the divisional detectives during the melee. But the plan, if it can be described as such, worked and that was all that mattered. There simply wasn't a safer or easier way to resolve the situation. For my part, having written my statement, the job was done and, along with my neighbour, we went back out on patrol. We celebrated breakfast in a local hospital canteen later that morning before finishing our shift and handing over to the next team.

Returning home that morning it was hard to comprehend the experiences of the night. Sleep came easily, probably as a result of the nervous energy expended. But for a few weeks my mind flashed back to the incident every now and again and the sight of Harkins standing outlined at the top of the stairs watching our arrival.

It later transpired that Harkins had previously attacked his wife and that police had been called to deal with his violent attacks against her. At the time of the murders, Harkins should have been in a psychiatric ward in Woodilee Hospital, near Glasgow, but had managed to slip out unnoticed. He had then gone to the Glasgow Royal Infirmary mortuary, where he had worked previously, and stolen a scalpel. Armed with his scalpel, Harkins had made his way to Gartnavel to carry out his vicious, horrific killings. The bloodstained scalpel was found in his jacket pocket when we arrested him in the Thornliebank flat.

This terrible night was one of the many occasions that I wondered what had led me to becoming a police officer. Throughout my career, there were many things that made me realise that, whatever had led me to join the police force, I had stumbled into a life that suited me so well. This was a job where I could sometimes make things right for people, at a moment in their lives when they were most in need. That wet, miserable night in February was just one of so many occasions.

2
Growing up in Partick

For a lively five-year-old boy, life in a Glasgow tenement in Partick in 1955 was a series of adventures. There were closes and back courts to explore and lots of other children to play with. Our home was in Fordyce Street and the families living there were working class. Most of the men were employed in the shipbuilding and railways industries that dominated the city of Glasgow, a vibrant city of the Empire with more than a million people living and working across the city's villages of Govan, Partick, Pollokshaws and the likes. For me, however, the city was made up of just half a dozen streets around my home.

Although I wasn't aware of it then, the most pressing worry for all these families was poverty. At that time few women worked, although some were 'lucky' enough to have domestic cleaning jobs in the nearby wealthier houses in Hyndland. The men, if working, were employed as labourers in low-skilled occupations building the ships, trains and railways that drove the economic prosperity of Glasgow.

The Pearson family lived in a single-bedroomed tenement flat on the second floor at number 23 Fordyce Street. The close mouth leading from the street was like most in the area, well looked after and washed and cleaned weekly by the two families on the ground floor. Each flight of stairs above were similarly swept and washed by one of the families resident on the floor above the flight. On the second-level landing of the close stood an outside toilet shared between the two families from the landing above. If you were lucky, toilet paper was provided from previous day's newspapers. It was important that each adult played their part in maintaining the good order of life in the close. Failing to pull your weight would mean conflict and argument between the women of the close. This usually ended with the miscreant caving in to the community pressure to conform and sticking to the unwritten rules of tenement-close living.

Our second floor home had the usual wooden front door with a small, coloured glass insert and a single Yale lock and it could also be bolted from inside. Its hallway – the lobby – was small and L-shaped with the living area/kitchen to the right with its single window overlooking the back court. The bedroom was on the left of the hallway with a window looking on to the street. This small, simple place was home for me and my mother and father.

On the opposite side of the landing lived the Scanlons. The father, Wee Jimmy, was a lamplighter. A small slim man, he was extremely dapper with a small pencil-line moustache. I rarely saw him during the day as he obviously worked nights. When I did see him in the close or the street he was usually carrying a small brass and wooden pole to light the gas lamps in closes across Glasgow. He was always quiet and reserved and left the talking to his wife, Rosie, who was a loud and substantial woman so typical of the housing schemes across Scotland. She was a rough woman to those who did not know her, but she was extremely supportive of this intimate community. A mother of two, she was never one to avoid sounding off on any subject. Over the years I came to know that should the need arise the Scanlons could be relied on to help in any emergency. In those days each family kept themselves to themselves and coped privately with the trials of poverty and the challenge of making ends meet.

9

My two best pals at the time were Hughie and Davie. They lived in nearby closes and we played together in the street. Some days we would be jumping the dykes in the back courts of Fordyce, Chancellor and Hyndland Streets where we each tried to prove our courage and show our contempt for danger. Often such adventures ended in injury for one of the band as some of the jumps between walls and dykes were too challenging. On quieter days we would join up with the rest of the street urchins playing hide-and-seek, 'kick the can' or street football. These games could go on till teatime or sundown depending on the weather, the availability of a tea worth going home for or a parent at home to look after you. Looking back, it was a carefree life which gave us a tremendous amount of freedom away from parents and the trials of life and poverty.

But the carefree life couldn't last forever and, for me, it ended abruptly with the start of school. My first school was St Peter's Primary in nearby White Street. Some of my friends went there with me at the same time while others went to the local Protestant school. I had no idea what that was. All I knew was that it meant that some of my friends attended a school somewhere else and although I didn't realise it at the time, the schism created by religion had entered my life for the very first time.

St Peter's was run by nuns. From the beginning my luck ensured that school was an experience I would rather forget. During the first few weeks, playing a game of hide-and-seek in the school playground, I had the bright idea to hide in the open-air toilet stalls and to stand on the basin rim of the toilet seat. It was an old trick that I'd often seen in the movies when the goodie or the baddie were hiding from one another. However, I hadn't planned on the poor maintenance of the school's toilet facilities. As soon as I had stepped up on to the porcelain block it cracked wide open and split down the middle. With water pouring from the bowl, I jumped off the wreckage of the toilet and bolted from the stall – but not before I'd been spotted by some other kids from the class.

It soon turned into a major incident. As soon as playtime finished, the teacher took our whole class aside to investigate the vandalism. She asked who had been responsible for the damage and began to question the class. It was a race to see who would name the culprit first amongst that group of five year olds. I didn't know whether or not to admit it or if I should just wait until the finger was pointed. In any case, the next thing I remember was being dragged by the jersey through the desks by the nun with her black habit flowing and being slapped about the ear and head as I was being propelled along the corridor. On the way to the head nun's office, we passed the large religious statue that stood sternly in the corridor, and each of these severe-looking figures seemed to be looking down in condemnation of what we'd done.

Alongside me was my friend Hughie who had also been in the toilet area but, as far as I can remember, played no part in the disaster. Both of us were wailing like wild animals as we were subjected to blows from behind. The threat of God's intervention hung in the air around us until finally we were abandoned to the head nun who left us in no doubt that we were evil boys and that our cards were marked. It was the final threat that our parents would be summoned to school the next day and asked to pay for the damage which sent a chill down our spines. This threat was the worst of all. Even at that young age, Hughie and I both knew our respective parents could not afford to pay for the damage.

We were both to be sent home with notes summoning our parents to school the next day. Seeing my mother at the school gates at 3pm that day with a nun by her side explaining to her what I had done, my life seemed at an end. For weeks afterwards, my simple home life was badly upset.

Eventually, things started to return to normal – thankfully without the need for a payment to the school – though from then onwards going to school and being taught by the nuns was never again such a happy prospect.

After a couple years at St Peter's Primary School, the boys transferred to St Peter's Boys' School in nearby Stewartville Street whilst the girls remained in White Street. At this time my father, Jim Pearson, worked as a carter for British Rail. Before that he had been a traceboy for a couple of years. A trace is either of the two straps or chains connected to a horse's harness which allows it to pull something. A traceboy's horse pulls another horse to help it with its load. My father had an undying love for horses, particularly Clydesdales. As a young boy of twelve, he was employed guiding a horse up the many hills in Glasgow's city centre, supporting the workhorses as they strove to pull their laden carts. At the top of each hill, the traceboy returned to the bottom with his horse to help the next cart. By the time I was aware of my father's work, he was a carter in his own right and one who took the care of his horses very seriously and was a trophy winner in the annual competitions. However, the changing world soon caught up with him and horses were no longer used for deliveries around Glasgow. My father was then transferred from the carthorses to work as a labourer laying track for British Railways on the west coast of Scotland.

For him this change was a disaster. Not only did he lose the job that he loved but he was paid less for working at a job that demanded a significant physical effort in harsh environments. It wasn't long before he started to join the rest of the crew and took to drinking heavily at the end of the working week.

One of my clearest memories of this period is of my father taking me to Buchanan Street Railway Station for a prize giving. He had won a Rose Bowl for the best turned-out horse in Scotland. The photographs of the time record the smart turnout, not only for the horse, but for all the Pearsons.

Typically I remember my father walking along Dumbarton Road in Partick at 5pm with his best workmate, Nelson Wright, and hundreds of shipyard and other workers at the end of their shift. Every Friday, wage packets in their pockets, most of these men made their way to the many public houses to wash away the dirt of the week. Often many of them were also drinking in preparation for an overtime shift on the nightshift that same evening. In either case it wasn't unusual to see women accosting their husbands in the streets or at the doors of the pubs trying to intercept the wage packet before it was all spent.

The next few years were interspersed for us with episodes during which my father drank heavily. This left the family short of cash and led to open warfare between my parents. By the time I was ten the situation had turned so violent that I was often chased out the house by my mother to save me from the unhappy sight of my parents arguing. When that happened, I was sent to the Scanlons or even to the pictures to keep me away from the unpleasant scenes but I was never oblivious to the atmosphere and could see the evidence of what had gone on behind closed doors from the occasional broken furniture, glass or, on one evening, the kitchen window.

When the back windowpane was broken I was off school with a broken collarbone. I had been playing in the streets as usual one Sunday evening when my pals and I had decided to climb the barriers at the front of the local St Peter's Church. Trying to be too smart, I climbed like Tarzan only to fall heavily on to the steps of the church. The pain was immediate and severe. I realised I had broken a bone and, of course, I knew the reception I would get at home. It also reinforced in my young mind that religion and I were to be uneasy bedfellows for life.

Once home from the hospital, complete with my sling, I had to be left during the day on my own as my mother was now working at the Southern General Hospital. I was duly warned about opening doors to strangers and behaving myself and Rosie Scanlon across the landing was usually on hand if needed. At some point in the day I was so bored that I decided to look out of the broken pane of glass into the back court. I climbed on to a chair and stood on the low sink in front of the window ledge. After pulling back the net curtain I put my head through the gap in the glass to see into the backcourt. I hadn't understood that in so doing I was up on my tiptoes and by the time I realised that I was seeing nothing of great interest (and in any case I was a bit frightened of heights) I no longer had the strength in my feet to ease up high enough to extract my face from the broken window and return to the room. To this day I remember the fear of hanging there, my body supported by a broken window held in place by a rotten window frame. I had lost my balance, the glass was digging into my neck and the window frame was the only thing supporting my body and stopping me from falling into the back court. The back court was about forty feet below but with each minute the height seemed to grow. It felt like I was stuck there for hours and I was crying hysterically. However, I think I was only really stuck for a few minutes before my mother returned to the house and rescued me. What a fool I felt and what a fright I got. My mother had also got such a fright that I didn't even get into trouble. However, the fear of heights has remained with me ever since.

When I was off school due to the broken collar bone, I answered the front door to be met by a photographer. Goodness knows what was said but I thought that there was some arrangement to take my photograph. I was duly snapped on the front doorstep as I stood there with a look of surprise and with my arm still in a sling. I forgot all about the photographer and didn't think to tell my parents about his visit. Then, a few weeks later, an envelope arrived at the house with the photograph and a bill for the photographer's services. Once again, my mother was not exactly delighted by the surprise although she did pay up and kept the photograph.

Although I wasn't privy to my parents' decision-making, I could see that my mother was taking control of the household finances and she also began studying to try to obtain professional nursing qualifications. At the same time my father appeared to display increasingly chaotic behaviour due to his excessive drinking. Despite our growing financial difficulties, on one occasion I recall him turning up at the house with a bouquet of flowers and on another Friday I remember he bought himself a new tailored suit to be paid for on credit. From time to time he took my mother and me to visit his mother's house in Govan. If one of his brothers was there he would often end up drunk and start fighting with them in the street. My lasting memory of one such visit was of two fried eggs sliding slowly down the kitchen wall having been thrown by one of the brothers during a fight.

Life at that time was not all like that, though. When sober, my father was the kindest and most thoughtful of people. He only ever struck me once in my life and that was when I was a teenager. And during these early years he would often come to the school gates at lunchtime and take me for a real coffee and something to eat at the local Italian café or teach me to ride my bike. On one occasion my father and I were cycling along South Street trying to avoid both the traffic and the railway lines in the roadway. Trains used the street to move equipment between the Albion Works, other factories and various storage sites. My father was so intent on making sure I was cycling carefully that he forgot to look after himself and caught the front wheel of his bike in the tracks and fell on to the road, cutting his nose and face. He was a real sight and it took weeks before my mother stopped ribbing him about his clumsiness. It was also the last time he took me out on a bicycle.

3

Taking on the School Bully

My years at St Peter's were spent with a mixed bunch of kids.
At one end of the class were the Elsbies – a large family of
boys who thankfully did not often turn up for school. With
hindsight I came to realise that, rather than being a family
of thugs and thieves, they were just one of the very poorest
families in the area. These kids were so poor that they rarely
changed their clothes or even washed and they had even
been known to come to school wearing their mother's boots.
The boots, a type of winter bootee, were made of black cloth
with a zip at the front and a wool lining inside. However,
when an Elsbie came to school wearing a bootee, no one
made any comment. We simply wouldn't have dared – it
would have started a war. Also in my class was Goudie, one
of the school bullies. He was a large boy who just seemed
to enjoy picking on the weaker members of the school. In
between these two extremes, we had a range of boys from
all over the district, some even from Byres Road, a more
affluent part of the city.

Whatever the mix, my life at St Peter's Boys' School in
Stewartville Street was reasonably happy. At break time sixty
boys were always to be found chasing a ball around the small
play area which was bordered by a high wall and railings. Just
about everyone took part in the game as it was the best way
to stay clear of the problem boys at the school – the bullies
and the misfits – who hung around looking for trouble.

For the most part I had been successful in keeping out of the way of the bullies. On one day, however, Goudie, who was big, heavy and enjoyed knocking boys around, had other ideas. He lived near the school but even out of school hours I kept well away from him. However, in my final months at St Peter's I somehow rubbed Goudie up the wrong way and it quickly became apparent that he had his sights set on me. Then, one lunch break, the moment came. Goudie had contrived to challenge me over something or other in front of most of my class and it was a put up or shut up time. If I was to walk away from the challenge I would be labelled a coward forever. To this day I don't know where it came from but I collected all the courage I could manage and flew at Goudie throwing everything I could at him – feet, fists, my head and anything else I could muster. The playground erupted with the excitement of a fight. The boys formed a ring around the two of us as we punched and gouged at each other. Suddenly it was all over when the janitor appeared from nowhere and separated us.

My face and ears were stinging not just from the bloody cuts around my mouth and nose but also from my red face, caused by my extreme embarrassment. I was also crying, as much through nerves and adrenalin as the pain. Having separated us, the janitor dragged us off and took us below the school building to the basement door leading to the head teacher's office. He pushed Goudie into one set of toilets to clean his face. I was pleased to see that I had managed to cut him and bruising was already starting to show around his eyes. I was sent into another toilet block to clean up but, as the janitor closed the door behind me, he congratulated me on my efforts. He knew very well that Goudie had been asking for it for a long time.

I had mixed emotions as I cleaned myself up. I feared what the head teacher would do to me and I was concerned what my parents would say when I arrived home in a state.

I also wondered what Goudie was thinking and what he would do next. However, I was quite pleased with myself as I'd survived the test and, although the result was painful, it wasn't half as bad as I imagined it was going to be.

The headmaster belted both of us, but not before he had lectured us about secondary school and our duty to behave properly. He then made Goudie and me shake hands. After the fight Goudie stayed away from me and thankfully I never had to worry about him again. In the playground I found I had suddenly acquired a reputation as a fighter – something I neither wanted nor cultivated. I just wanted to be left alone to get on with my life.

When I got home that afternoon, I handed over the headmaster's note and got the expected lecture about my behaviour from my mother and some dire warnings about where I would end up if I did not get a grip of myself by the time my father came home. Apart from a few jokes about the state I was in, nothing more was said. I had nevertheless learned a valuable lesson – bullies could be confronted and forced to go away. It was a lesson that would stay with me throughout my adult life.

Having sat my eleven-plus exams, I was told that I had done enough to win a place at St Mungo's in the East End, academically a well-regarded school. The headmaster at St Peter's, Mr Ribchester, sent for my parents after the results were announced. He advised them that it would be better for all concerned if another boy at my school went to St Mungo's whilst I should go to St Thomas Aquinas Secondary School. The other boy's father had recently died and Mr Ribchester believed that the boy would benefit from going to St Mungo's and that I would do fine at either school. My parents agreed, largely, I am certain, because they lacked the confidence to challenge the head teacher.

4
My First Run-in with the Police

It was around this time I had my first contact with the police. Friday nights had become tense at home as my mother waited to see if my father would turn up at teatime and what kind of state he'd be in. My mother had extended her hours to help pay the family's way and I have little doubt she was increasingly frustrated by his behaviour. One Friday my father had failed to appear and, as we waited for him and his wages, it was evident that my mother was becoming desperate. Rosie from across the landing had provided supper that night as it was already 8pm. She understood the problems we faced as Rosie also had similar difficulties – few households in the street were exempt. I was dispatched to the corner shop to get some food on credit to see us through. The local shopkeeper, who lived in the rear of the shop in Fordyce Street, was sympathetic. I was given some basics – bread, tea, milk and, I suppose, cigarettes. I remember wee Jimmy, the owner, marking up the debt in his journal before I left the shop. It was evident that we were up against it and that the family was in danger of disintegrating.

At 10pm father turned up drunk. He arrived at the door plainly keen for a friendly welcome and a quiet reception from my mother. I remember feeling sorry for him. Both my mother and I were tired. The strain of the long wait and the anxiety of the situation had taken its toll on both of us as my smiling father, his eyes deadened by the effects of alcohol, staggered through the lobby still wearing his work overalls. My mother suddenly unleashed her anger in a way I had not seen before. She screamed about his lack of care for his family and demanded to know where he had been, who with and how much money he had left. My father misread the position completely and tried to make light of the situation by telling her not to worry. It was the worst response he could have made. She was sick with worry and had suffered the embarrassment of sharing her financial difficulties with the neighbours and the local shopkeeper.

Without warning my mother went for my father's face and neck. Drunk or not, he easily knocked her aside. I stepped into the exchange to distract my father's attention at which point my mother caught him full in the face with her fist and knocked him through the lobby into the doorway of the bedroom and straight into the wardrobe door, smashing it to bits. The violence of those few seconds was shocking, though it owed as much to my father losing his balance and falling as it did to my mother's right hook. The most frightening part of it all came as I saw my father begin to gather himself from inside the wardrobe and try to get to his feet again. There was a lot of shouting and I don't know if I was told or decided it for myself, but I was soon on my way to the local police office.

I ran the two blocks to the police station at Gullane Street – the Marine police office – and burst through the swing doors to tell whoever was present that my mother needed the police (although as of the last exchange I had seen it was more likely my father needed them). I remember the strange mixture of emotions I felt at the police office. The office seemed so calm and under control. The man behind the desk appeared utterly unfazed by my arrival and my rush of excitement, fear and worry about what was about to happen to my family. He'd seen it all many times before, of course. Two uniform constables soon appeared from behind the desk and led me back home.

Since my departure, more furniture had been broken and there was blood all over the bedroom. Both my parents looked the worse for their exchanges and my mother was distraught. The policemen took control, instructing Mrs Scanlon to take me into her house, while they went into my home to sort out the mess. Half an hour later I was taken back home. My father was no longer there and my mother was sitting alone in the kitchen, crying her eyes out. My father had been taken by the police and was to be locked up. The contents of his pockets had been emptied on to the kitchen table to help keep us for the weekend, though there was not much there. My mother was worried about what would become of us all. How could we pay any fine that might be imposed and how could we survive at all if my father was jailed? My mother and I gathered ourselves together and tidied up as best we could before going to bed. I felt a sense of shame that I had been involved in getting my father locked up. At the same time I was worried about what would become of him if he was locked up overnight in a police cell. It was an accepted truth in our streets that the police would give you a good kicking once you were inside the police office. Whatever the rights and wrongs of what had happened that night, I still loved my father and I didn't want him to suffer. Nevertheless, I was struck by the ability of the police officers to take control of the situation and sort it out.

When we woke up on the Saturday morning I knew that my life was going to change. My mother told me we didn't have enough money to last the week, never mind pay any fine. The prospect of a fine seemed particularly unjust in the circumstances given our lack of cash. Mrs Scanlon came in to see us and advised that my father was bound to be fined as he had not been in trouble before. It was clear that though she would help us as best she could Rosie Scanlon had no more money than we had. She would share what food she could but her offer of support was all the more degrading to my mother given our circumstances.

Like most other Partick families we had no telephone and no way to contact those who might help us. My mother decided that we needed to resolve the immediate problems and for the only time in my life that I remember we walked to the nearby pawnshop in Purdon Street. I don't know what we had to pawn but, when we got upstairs to the first-floor shop, the cubicle you sat in to discuss the transaction was so small that we couldn't both fit inside. I think it may have been jewellery she pawned but as a result of our visit to the pawnshop we had enough to keep us going in the short term. There was even enough for a treat and the two of us went to the local picture house during the late afternoon before buying chips for supper that evening. An escape to a warm cinema lost in someone else's drama was the perfect answer to our needs that day.

On Sunday afternoon, I was dispatched to Nelson Wright's house to ask him to cover for my father's absence at work the next day. Nelson was a great friend to my father, although I'm sure he encouraged all his misadventures. I could see, even late on the Sunday, that Nelson was still recovering from the excesses of the weekend. His wife, Bella, had decided that, if you could not beat your husband's behaviour, you could only join him. Nelson immediately understood my father's problem and told me he would make sure all would be well at work. My father would be reported as being off sick to give him time to get himself together. Presumably he'd have lost pay, however, and there was much talk about Dad having to get back to work as soon as possible.

On the Monday, I was sent to school as usual although it was the last place I wanted to go to. By the time I arrived home from school, Dad was sitting in the kitchen. The atmosphere in the house was nonetheless sombre and there was very little talk. I felt a great relief that he was home but loyalty to my mother meant I could not display my feelings. My father for his part looked a sorry soul. Usually bright, smart and ever ready to smile, he now looked old, depressed and subdued.

It was at least an hour before I realised he could not get up from his seat. It became obvious when he wanted a wash. His legs were unable to carry him. Finally he took off his socks and I saw that both his feet were so swollen he could not put his boots on. He had appeared at the court shoeless and, having received the usual lecture from the magistrate, had been fined. He had then walked home from the police office carrying his boots. There were cuts and bruises everywhere.

By his account, coloured of course by his drunkenness, he had been frogmarched by the police officers to the station where he was told to remove his working boots before being locked up in a cell. An argument and a struggle with the officers led him to receive a beating around his feet. If he couldn't get his boots on, my father couldn't go to work and he couldn't earn. In any case, his condition was a result of his own foolishness as far as my mother was concerned. His behaviour had embarrassed the family, left us almost penniless and put our future at risk. His feet were in a terrible mess though.

I was too angry with him to care much about how he came by his injuries. I just wanted a stable home and loving parents. What I had was a family at war. It was many years later before I saw for myself how such injuries might have occurred. Years later, I'd often lock up drunk and violent people. Every prisoner had their belt and shoes removed before being placed in a cell. How often I saw men in bare feet lying on the cell floor or merely standing at the cell door kicking at solid metal for hours on end, demanding to be released. I even saw a man kick a porcelain toilet bowl to pieces with his bare feet in one police office. I like to think that my father could not come home after that night in the cells and admit his additional folly to my mother.

One way to escape from these experiences was joining the cubs and then the scouts. At least once a week and sometimes at weekend camps, I was involved in a planned, organised and satisfying way of life. Almost from the beginning I enjoyed the cubs and the costs of joining were minimal. Every Wednesday night, along with about forty others, I returned to school at 6.30pm and for a couple of hours would play games, learn skills and become involved in planning projects. It was a real freedom. The men and women who led the pack were always supportive and gave each of us a real sense of worth and accomplishment. Near the end of my time in the cubs I was taken with the pack to stay overnight at Auchingillan Camp. We stayed overnight under canvas, cooked our own meals and cleaned the plates using grass. What an adventure for a city boy. I'm sure my parents also benefited from my absence allowing them some space in our small house to try and resolve their differences. By the time I joined the Scouts (141st Glasgow) I was identified as an organiser. Looking back its almost unbelievable, given our modern experience, that cubs and scouts were actually encouraged to go round strange streets and houses volunteering to do work in exchange for contributions during bob-a-job week. I loved it and the feeling of being useful and contributing to something bigger than my own mundane life was extremely satisfying.

One visit to our cub pack was to have a huge impact on me. The chance to meet and even shake hands with Celtic goalkeeper Ronnie Simpson has remained with me all my life. Here was an ordinary working-class boy who went on to become a world-class goalkeeper and who showed that it was possible for ordinary boys to achieve the extraordinary. With his visit and talk he provided a massive boost to my own ambitions.

My second means of escape was to meet up with my pals and play around the streets. One Friday evening, four of us met to compare home life and we had managed to collect together enough money to buy a bottle of 'scoosh' or lemonade. As it was a Friday, we decided to buy something unusual. Vimto, American Cream Soda and Tizer were our usual tipples but this time we bought a bottle of soda water thinking it was a grown-up drink. Four youngsters then sat on the high pavement outside the Hyland Bar in Fordyce Street ready to enjoy our luxury together only to discover that the taste was disgusting. We tried to take it back to the shop and explain we had made a mistake but the café owner showed us the door. We were left to pour most of it down the drain so that at least we could claim the thruppence back on the empty bottle.

On another Friday evening, my father came home late from the pub and I was sent round to Mr Abrami's, our local chip shop in Hyndland Street. It would have been about 10pm and, as usual, the shop was full of a mix of people. As I joined the back of the queue, I could see drunken men still dressed in their dirty work clothes, teenagers a few years older than me sharing a bag of chips and older locals, collecting their evening meal.

Abrami's was always a welcoming family-run shop, with father, mother and son working behind a high, stone counter opposite the front door and Formica walls, which were cleaned daily. There was a large plate-glass window at the front of the shop which allowed passers-by to see in.

This evening the shop was livelier than usual. Quite a few of the customers had been drinking and there was a lot of loud banter and the occasional few bars of a song. Mr Abrami didn't like noise in his chip shop but with the Friday crowd he found it difficult to keep the usual good order.

As I waited impatiently at the back of a queue of about twenty-five people, two youngsters came in behind me. It was obvious that they had been drinking and they had a mean, troubled look about them. Although only about seventeen, they were both well known locally as thieves and housebreakers.

These two, and others who always hung about the corner of Fordyce Street, were responsible for much of the crime in the area but nothing ever seemed to happen to them. When not standing on the street corner, the gang would roam the area looking for trouble and starting fights. Often they would target students passing through the area on their way to Glasgow University.

On this night, I could sense there was going to be trouble when these two swaggered into the chip shop. There was a flicker of recognition in the eyes of the smaller of the two when he saw me at the back of the queue but he looked past me into the crowd. I watched as both men homed in on a teenage couple in the middle of the queue.

The couple, who were smartly turned out, looked as if they were finishing their evening date with a bag of chips when these two drunks came right up to them. They said something to the girl, which I couldn't quite make out, but I knew instinctively what was coming.

The girl was pretty and, as her partner didn't belong to the area, these two neds had decided they were going to teach him a lesson and show off to their audience. As the young man responded to the taunts, I could see that he had realised he was in trouble.

The only way out was past the troublemakers and behind him were strangers and the high-sided counter. Trapped, with his girlfriend between him and the men, I could sense the fear emanating from him. Suddenly the two neds attacked the young man, throwing his girlfriend out of the way. Within seconds, the mood in Abrami's shop had changed from a boisterous happy evening to one of shock and horror. The two kicked, punched and slashed their victim. It was all over in less than a minute but that minute has remained engrained in my memory. What was so shocking was the callous and inhuman way these two thugs treated this young man.

Mrs Abrami started screaming as the men launched their attack. Her husband, armed with a brush, came round to the public side of the counter but before he had arrived, the two men had completed their work and walked casually out of the shop, as if nothing had happened.

Behind they left chaos. The young woman was distraught and concerned for her partner, who was trying to stem the blood gushing from his face. While some in the queue didn't want to get involved, a couple of young men were angry at what had happened. As the Abramis helped the injured man, I realised there was no point in waiting for food and returned home to tell my mother what had happened.

Although I hadn't been threatened, my mother never again sent me out for food late in the evening. It was also made clear to me that I should never get involved with this group of youngsters, who were seen as a threat to all decent-minded people in the area.

The next afternoon, I saw the two attackers standing, with their gang, in their usual place on the corner of Fordyce Street. It was less than fifty metres from the chip shop. I just couldn't believe these two could stand openly in a public place, just hours after committing such a horrible and cowardly act. As I walked past, neither of them looked at me. They believed they were in charge of the streets. It was only when the police came around that these thugs and bullies disappeared.

During the day my friends and I often gathered to play war games. In the late 1950s, we were able to find old equipment abandoned in the area – ammunition boxes, gas masks and the likes. As a gang we would gather up the stuff and walk up the hill to an open site we called the Bumble Bee, north of the park at Highburgh Road. My parents never did find out exactly where the Bumble Bee was. Today it has houses built on it but in the late 50s and early 60s it was a place where we could hide in the long grass and bushes and fight out 'wars'. Across from the site were the rear windows of terraced houses and many an afternoon I was at the Bumble Bee with a couple of my friends when piano music or singing could be heard coming from the nearby houses. It was live music, practice sessions, wafting across the open ground. I often remember lying in the grass listening to the music with the heat of the sun radiating over my face as I waited for the assault due from my pals as they sought to take the high ground at the rear of the Bee. Families living in these houses experienced a very different life from my own. As a Scout I visited these houses as much out of interest as anything else. Jimmy Logan, the famous music hall figure, lived in one of them – he chased me away and told me not to come back. As I got older, I still loved going up to the Bumble Bee as it was a place of real peace and tranquillity and you were never harassed but with secondary school beckoning, everything was about to change.

We had lived in the same house for as long as I could remember and it was a big shock to be told we were moving home. Before we did, I brought one final crisis to the house on Fordyce Street. We had recently bought a small black and white television and one of my favourite habits was to watch the television in the kitchen while my mother cooked dinner. One time, I was sitting on the arm of a chair pretending to be in the *Lone Ranger* show when I suddenly jumped off the seat to ride off into the sunset at the end of the programme. Unfortunately for me, I rode straight into the frying pan which my mother was lifting towards the plates. The pain was so intense that I didn't even feel my skin burning. I wasn't certain if it was hot fat or cold water on my face – but it was extremely painful. My father wasn't at home and there was no one available to help. Thankfully, because of my mother's nursing experience, she knew what to do next. A cold wet towel was put on my face and my mother took a blanket from the bed, gathered me up in her arms and ran the quarter of a mile with me to the Western Infirmary. My mother was in a terrible state, crying and breathless due to the shock and the sheer physical effort of carrying me.

At the hospital I was rushed straight through to the casualty department and seen immediately by a doctor. The medical team began to remove skin and grease from my face and I finally began to feel the effects of the accident as the initial shock wore off. I could see that the last thing my mother needed was a hysterical child on her hands. A couple of hours later my father turned up at the hospital from his work. The doctors had removed all the material that concerned them and they told my parents that I would be unlikely to suffer any ill effects. Thankfully they were right and I owe them a great deal for the way in which they looked after me that night.

Needless to say, another lecture was forthcoming once the panic was over and I never again joined in the television stories when Mum was cooking. Shortly after, we were on the move – to a bigger flat just around the corner in Chancellor Street. The Pearsons were going upmarket.

5
The Long and Winding Road to the Police

My new school, St Thomas Aquinas in Scotstoun, was built as the result of the fresh approach to comprehensive education in the 1960s. A huge combined junior and secondary school, it had nearly 2,000 pupils from all over the west side of Glasgow. No account was taken of the territorialism so prevalent in Glasgow at that time and still in existence to this day. Young men and women at a crucial time in their development could end up facing gangs of youths from the wrong area in the wrong location. It was not uncommon for fights to break out during or immediately after school. Prefects did well to avoid involvement in these disturbances and, on a number of occasions, pupils were badly assaulted or slashed. I teamed up with a group of boys from Partick. We met in the morning in Dumbarton Road outside the library, taking the number 6 bus to the Jordanhill side of the school. We could have taken other buses to the Scotstoun side of the site but that meant passing through Whiteinch and Scotstoun with the chance we could meet up with the boys from Yoker.

My huge school lacked character and felt more like an education factory but many of the teachers were excellent and worked hard to motivate their slovenly charges in difficult circumstances. My key teachers were Mr Docherty in English (aka 'Nose' due to his prominent neb); Mr Besant in French and Mr McGhee, also in the French department. Sometimes I thought that McGhee could be a particularly unpleasant teacher, aggressive and keen to deprecate his charges. He nonetheless seemed to care and demonstrated all the frustration of a teacher who understood the difficulties faced by many of his pupils and wanted to drive them to achieve and to better themselves.

Regularly on a Friday afternoon, instead of teaching French, he would lecture us on the hurdles to overcome in facing the future – a future he believed was there for us to seize. Nose Docherty was far too subtle for such protestations but he introduced me to the pleasures of reading Shakespeare, Coleridge and the essayists. Although he was fairly small and slight, he always wore his academic gown and occasionally, I'm sure, wore his mortar board. Of all teachers it was his lessons that made the difference for me and I became an avid reader by second year. A reader influenced by the events of the time, JFK, the Cuban missile crisis, and trade union disputes in Britain as the ideas of Marx, Rousseau and Coleridge fired my imagination.

At the same time, things at home were changing. My father accepted his behaviour could not be tolerated and finally decided it was time to face up to his demons. We had lived in Chancellor Street for more than a year with the flat's larger rooms and improved environment. There was an air of comparative affluence about the house. We even managed to have a holiday to Ayr. Nevertheless my father still had occasional trips with his friends to the pub. It was obvious that he couldn't help himself. Something had to be done.

My parents decided that my father needed medical treatment for his condition. Initially that meant him attending the doctor and receiving medication but it soon became evident that he was going to have to go to hospital.

But my father did not want to go. He had been an inpatient as a child and had been well aware that some patients didn't survive, a fear that had remained with him. I also knew that he didn't enjoy mixing with strangers. Although a relaxed and engaging sort, he had little in the way of small talk and felt inferior to others due to his lack of education. I think that's why he enjoyed the company of his horses so much. It gave him the opportunity to be the best at something and he was more relaxed in their company. There was nothing else for it and my father left us to go to a ward in the Southern General.

He left the house on a Monday morning, dressed in his best suit, collar and tie. He looked extremely worried but promised to be home by the weekend. As it turned out, however, he was away for more than a month. For the first week, I received updates on his progress from my mother but it took a while to persuade her to let me visit the hospital. The following Sunday my mother and I took the subway to Govan and walked over to the hospital. My mother was dressed in her best Sunday clothes and wore full make-up. In those days the fashion was for make-up to be almost mask-like with layers of foundation, panstick, lipstick and rouge. There was no mistaking her nervousness, a nervousness that transferred to me as we got close to Dad's ward.

Dad was in the psychiatric section of the hospital which was always kept locked. We stood in the wind and cold for some minutes until a male nurse came to the door and, after peering through the reinforced glass insert, he unlocked the door and let us in. The corridor leading to the ward was uninviting and grubby with men standing alone and self-absorbed. A couple of them were talking to themselves and one was weeping but no one paid any attention to his misery. My mother and I followed the male nurse to a waiting area. There was a horrible stench in the ward. It wasn't dirt but a combination of tobacco smoke and sweat. The furniture was cheap, badly chipped and covered with cigarette burns.

The nurse told my mother that my father was responding well to his treatment but as we walked into the waiting area I was shocked to see the change in him. He hardly looked liked the man I had seen a week earlier. His hair was wild and dishevelled, his face grey and gaunt and his clothing was grubby. It was his eyes that frightened me most – they were empty and lifeless. My father barely seemed to recognise us and I felt that he only tried to recognise us because he was frightened and he needed someone, anyone, to care for him. I presume it was the medication that had affected him. He was so confused that I had to convince him about the life he had outside the hospital. He did not seem persuaded by my explanations. His condition clearly frightened my mother, who found it difficult to maintain a conversation during our stay.

After barely half an hour we were ready to leave and the nurse who had stayed in the room throughout the visit was equally keen to show us the door. As we rose to leave, my father panicked and made it clear that he did not want us to leave without him. He was scared and childlike in the way he showed that fear without embarrassment or self-consciousness. Like my mother, I found my father's exhibition of emotions embarrassing and extremely upsetting. We both felt we had abandoned my father when he needed us most. We could only hope it was all for the best. Things would not improve for some time.

As we left the hospital, it must have seemed an impossible situation for my mother. Stuck with a young boy, a husband who was in no state to play his part in the family or the marriage, she must have had a sense of foreboding in her mind. For my part I was in a dreadful turmoil. I hadn't expected a fun afternoon but to see my father in such a frightened state caused me immense anxiety and unhappiness.

Life in the Pearson household marked time as my mother and I struggled to maintain some sense of normality.

Some weeks later, I learned that Dad was to be allowed home for the weekend. As the Friday afternoon came, I couldn't get home quickly enough from school. As I arrived I saw that he was already home but he was not my father. What I saw was the shell of someone I used to know as my father. Here was a man who had undergone electric shock treatment at the hands of the doctors trying to making him well again but they had destroyed his very essence and replaced it with emptiness and pain. His eyes were lifeless. He did not recognise me or my mother and he was afraid of anything and everything. My mother and I had a stranger at home. It was awful. By eight o'clock that evening my father, who had been so vibrant and fun-loving, was reduced to getting ready for bed like an exhausted child. His sole interest appeared to be chain-smoking cigarettes.

At two o'clock in the morning I was woken by my mother who was troubled by my father's behaviour. He had awoken from sleep, apparently unaware of his whereabouts and had begun to wander round the flat, clearly disorientated. He wanted to go back to work on the railways. By the time I had dressed, my father was outside the front door in his pyjamas walking down the stairs looking for something he might recognise and understand. It was only by joining him in the close and telling him repeatedly who I was and that I loved him that I was able to persuade him to return to our flat. In his troubled state he needed someone to love him and he needed to sleep. With my mother's support he found some peace of mind and finally went back to sleep. By Monday morning we were all exhausted and, in truth, glad to see father back to the safety of the hospital ward. I could not understand what had been done to my father and why. I could only hope that things would work out for the best.

Thankfully, within the month, my father was deemed to

have responded to the treatments. Years later he would tell me of his fear at being led to the treatment room where he would have wires connected to his skull and electric shock treatments (EST) administered. At the same time he had a new drug pumped into his system, 'Antabuse', a wonder chemical designed to work alongside the EST to remove the desire to drink. It says much for his strength of character that at the conclusion of his time at the hospital he had stopped drinking and would never drink again. The change in him was all the more remarkable because he still went to the pub with his mates but just didn't drink.

It was around this time that he also began to fill the large gaps in his education. I discovered he could barely read and couldn't do arithmetic. Together we began to learn the basic skills of literacy and numeracy at the kitchen table. His main motivation to learn arose from a change in procedures at his work. He needed to be able to complete a timesheet each week outlining his hours, the nature of the work and the overtime due. He was unable to submit his timesheets but with my help he began to learn. By the end of the year he had overcome his inability to the extent that he was filling in not only his own timesheet but also the sheets for the rest of the crew. Eventually he rose to be appointed as a railway inspector but he never completely overcame his lack of education and I never forgot the inferiority he so obviously felt.

As the trauma of my father's illness subsided and I settled into secondary school, I started to get interested in the music scene. Popular music became a magnet to many youngsters attracted to the success and status it was afforded by the media. I was not alone in believing that I too could play a guitar and become successful. Adverts of the time showed that a Hofner guitar could be bought for fifty guineas and it was possible to learn to play it in weeks. I pestered my mother and father for a guitar and they bought me my first one through the post on hire purchase. The guitar arrived at Chancellor Street in a large cardboard box. Inside I found a beautiful red and black electric guitar with a shoulder strap, a plectrum and a study book to help learn the chords. I was delighted. I could neither tune the guitar nor play any chords but making the noise was good enough to begin with. My father was particularly keen for me to pursue music. He loved pop music and was constantly whistling 'Telstar' – the hit of the day by the Tornados. My mother was less enthusiastic. She feared I would lose interest in school and that my examination grades would be affected. Nevertheless she allowed me to take music lessons with a Mr Falconer who lived nearby in Mansfield Street. Either he was not a gifted teacher or, more likely, I was a poor student but I didn't get far with the music in the months I attended Mr Falconer's house on a Saturday morning.

My time with the Scouts was coming to an end as the activities lost their attraction for me. I began to take nights off, not because I was hanging about the streets but more because the Scouts were becoming boring – doing the same things week after week. I began to practise the guitar more regularly and started to think I was getting pretty good. I could play many of the tunes of the day but I had no band to play with. Soon I joined up with three boys from White Street and Hyndland Street to form a band. They were called the Bowmen and with Phil, Billy and Brian we started rehearsing our songs at various houses to begin with. From the start, my father appointed himself as the group's roadie and he helped find rooms for us to practise in and transport for our equipment. Before very long we were travelling right across the Central Belt playing in dance halls and at fetes. A small hall in Partick's Burgh Hall Street – adjacent to the railway station – became our practice place and young boys and girls gathered outside to listen to us play. It was a great time for the band. It was exciting to earn a little money and we were in demand as word of mouth spread about our performances. With the help of Billy and the others in the band, we bought an old Thames van. That old van took us all around Scotland and as far north as a dance hall in Macduff, to Strathaven in Lanarkshire and many of the towns and villages in between. At various times from the stage, I would watch gangs fighting in the dancehalls as police attended to bring peace. I was again impressed by the way officers could handle the neds.

It was tiring work, however. On one occasion, we played Perth Town Hall on a Thursday night and our performance was so well received that we couldn't get away until after midnight. After travelling to Glasgow and emptying the van it was the early hours before we got to bed. This routine became normal for the next year or so. My father, in his new sober state, loved it. He was extremely supportive and loved acting as roadie, manager and critic. My mother, though, became increasingly worried. Sometimes I was too tired to go to school and she also thought I was being drawn into the 'glamour' of the music scene. I could see a future for myself in a band, escaping the mundane world of working. If I wasn't going to be a star, though, I still had a hankering to join the police.

6

The Hard Life and Joining Up

Domestically, my home life had become settled. My mother worked hard at the Southern General to get her nursing qualifications while my father continued working on the railways. Finances were no longer the problem they had been for the previous five or six years. We might not have been affluent but as Prime Minister Harold Macmillan insisted: 'We've never had it so good.' Holidays became a new feature of our year and the three of us would trot off to Scarborough for a fortnight's break in Mrs Foster's bed and breakfast. We travelled on my father's free railway pass and every year stayed at the same digs, knowing that we would be well received, provided with good food and would have clean, quiet rooms. It was during these trips as a twelve-, thirteen- and fourteen-year-old that I would traipse around the shops watching my father enjoying his new passion of buying watches or rings for my mother. After the experiences they had come through they deserved some pleasure. Like any other youngster, I used to complain repeatedly that nothing was being bought for me. We would march around the shops for what seemed like hours, my mother and father arm-in-arm whilst I chanted incessantly: 'I want something . . . I get nothing . . . I want something . . . I get nothing . . .' As they walked behind me, I'm sure they were both quietly laughing at their stupid son and winding me up ever so gently by buying more and more things for themselves.

Each evening, we would walk along the seafront and have a supper or an ice cream before going back to Mrs Foster's. Often we would take in a show, Ken Dodd, Dickie Henderson and the like. These were holidays to remember. Although the wind on the east coast can be unforgiving – particularly with the haar – I remember only sunshine, camomile lotion and sunburned skin. We always returned to Glasgow by train and arrived home feeling refreshed and relaxed but looking forward to our next visit to Yorkshire.

Back home, I had started to get seriously involved in my music. I left the local band to join what I hoped would be a successful outfit. After travelling extensively around the United Kingdom with the new group it became obvious to me that I was unlikely to make a life in music. I'd left home before my seventeenth birthday to concentrate on music but I ran out of steam and, with barely any cash left, found myself in Nottingham. Leaving home had been a terrible trauma for the whole family. My mother had been completely against the idea but at the same time she could see no future for me in a band. I had been fortunate in the timing of my departure in that I had managed to sit my school examinations before going off with the band and had managed somehow to accumulate a range of passes at 'O' level. My father as always was very supportive of my desire to be a musician and though concerned at the prospect of my leaving home he did not stand in my way. Almost as I left home it became obvious that the band was beginning to fall apart as various members decided they had other interests to pursue.

The band having fallen apart, I found myself living in a rented flat in Nottingham. I needed to find a job and I was lucky to find one with a firm of chartered accountants. The senior partner was the appropriately named Mr Cashmore! I also took some work in a lounge bar as well as temping as a session guitarist at a local recording studio.

It was a tough time, though, as I slowly began to build my own life in a new city. Throughout this time, although my mother and father had been shocked at my departure, we all kept in contact. In fact, my father was dispatched at regular intervals to use his free railway pass to travel to Nottingham, check on my well-being and deliver money and support. With hindsight it must have been a particularly difficult time for both my parents as their only son set off, without ceremony, allegedly to make his way in the world, far from home.

After fourteen months of struggle during which time I had studied for further exams and built up a reasonable lifestyle, I knew it was time to return home to Glasgow and rekindle my interest in the police. Accountancy was not for me. I did enjoy balancing the books and visiting factories and farms to gather together the information for tax returns but I found an accountant's life stale and lacking in excitement. Back at home I returned to my old school to sit my Higher examinations and thankfully passed. It was also at this time I first set eyes on a young woman who was later to become my wife.

Around this time I approached the police about joining up. Initially my application was not well received – I was too young, not a member of a traditional police family and I had been brought up in a working-class area of Glasgow.

However, at that time my mother was nursing a senior police officer who was a patient at the Southern General. Mr Hyslop advised me that I should re-apply and he would ensure the application was given consideration. It was and I was given the chance to sit the entrance exam and be interviewed. Finally I was accepted for the Force but I would not be recruited until March 1970.

While awaiting my call-up, I spent the bitter autumn and winter of 1969–70 working on a building site in Cumbernauld. It turned out to be ideal training for the police. Every morning at six I was picked up by a service bus from St Enoch Square and dropped back there at six at night. I spent every day, which always seemed to be wet and cold, in the company of men who had no alternative but to take on this hard, demanding work.

At break time, covered in mud, we sat in silence to eat. The room was full of steam from a combination of the heat of our bodies and the propane heaters in the huts. Water ran down the hut windows and we rarely seemed to get a glimpse of daylight. It was dark when we started work, pitch black by the time we finished and in between I can remember only hard work. I drove a dumper truck around the site delivering concrete and cement to navvies working in teams. If the navvies were kept waiting for their deliveries it cost them their bonus and they were quick to express their displeasure. Most of the time this was verbal abuse but any worker who was deemed to be at it would be beaten up. In the silence of the breaks men sat reading newspapers, eating or just sleeping but rarely do I remember much fun or conversation – it was that kind of a place.

At one stage there was a strike over pay and working conditions. Most of the workers didn't want to go on strike as they could ill afford it. However, I was fascinated by the union meeting held on a site between the huts and how the votes could be manipulated to 'encourage' the outcome that the union leaders wanted. In this case, workers who did not support the strike were invited to leave the meeting and stand next to adjacent huts in full view of their colleagues. Very few workers were brave enough to walk out of the crowded meeting and those who did were subjected to verbal abuse and threats. I was just grateful that my working future lay elsewhere. After a few days the strike was over but the impact on relationships across the workforce was obvious. There was even talk that workers who hadn't supported the strike were likely to suffer more accidents but I saw no evidence of this.

I can still recall the trip back to Glasgow every night on the service bus which was little better than a cattle truck. Stuck on a hard seat with very little light, the bus took thirty tired, damp men home in silence every night. Most of the men just sat staring out the window at the rain and dark outside or slept – all in a world of their own.

Once at St Enoch I took the subway home to Partick Cross. I soon noticed that very few people would sit near me on the subway. I looked like a miner just back from the coal-face – my boots and clothes were covered in mud and my hair was thick with dirt which occasionally ran down my face and neck in streaks. Even my girlfriend wouldn't meet me in the street. Every night I enjoyed the luxury of a bath – without it life would have been unbearable. For many of my colleagues on the site, life was very different. They had no bath and spent most evenings sitting in the pub, still filthy from their day's hard labour.

I thought this tough, physical environment would be the perfect introduction to the police service and, after my months toiling at the building site, I was confident that nothing could test my resolve to the same extent. How wrong I was proved to be.

7

The Beat Generation

Just joining the City of Glasgow Police was an ordeal. Along with a dozen others, I turned up for my first day at police headquarters in St Andrew's Street in the Saltmarket. We had been told to report to the front desk at 9am where we assembled like new kids on their first day at school. There was just one woman and about a dozen men of all ages. A couple of the men were even younger than I was, having transferred directly from the cadets on their nineteenth birthday. The others were a variety of labourers and students and some who had found their old jobs uninteresting and had a hankering to join the police.

Once inside, I was sent into a large room and required to fill out endless forms about my next of kin, home address, bank details and so on. When this was finished the sergeant looking after us came in with another pile of forms to sign related to our future duties, insurance cover and pension matters. As we all began to sign the forms, the sergeant, suddenly and with a dramatic flourish, ordered us all to stop and warned us that we should never sign anything until we had read it. He warned us that the bureaucracy would 'steal' our rights if we were not careful. What a welcome to a new job! In this dim and distant era, long before the Edmund Davis police pay deal reformed conditions for the police, many officers felt they were treated badly. Hordes of officers were leaving the service because of the poor pay and conditions, taking jobs driving taxis where they'd earn much more than in the police.

The headquarters seemed to be an extremely busy building. As well as the administration staff, there was the criminal records office, forensic science officers and various detectives visiting HQ to collect records or obtain statements – or, as I learned later, hanging about the front door or the canteen just to be seen by the bosses.

Although there was only one canteen, there were a number of smaller rooms off the main seating area in which groups of mostly Highland men gathered, often talking in Gaelic. They were in their thirties and forties and were relaxed, laughing and chatting, as in any canteen across the land. However, there was something different about these people and it wasn't just the sight of the tunics and diced caps or the handcuffs and batons. I felt a real buzz of excitement in the air. As new recruits, we weren't yet a part of these special groups. The officers looked on us with curiosity while we stared back equally fascinated.

After our induction, we gathered in the canteen on the ground floor before heading over to the training school in Oxford Street. Leaving the headquarters, I recall vividly paying a visit to the ground-floor gents and being struck by the height of the coat hooks. As it soon became clear, I had joined a force of giants.

A week before I started the job, my father spoke to me. He had never interfered with anything I had wanted to do and, it soon became apparent, he had no intention of doing so now. However, he wanted me to be aware of the full implications and dangers of joining the police. Given his own working experience, he was concerned that I would not be able to cope with the physical and mental demands of the job. He was also unsure how the unusual sight of a uniformed police officer would be received in Chancellor Street and what this would mean for me, on and off duty.

My father just wanted to reassure himself that I had thought all these things through, which I had.

My only concern was that my parents would suffer or be abused, because I had joined the police. My father told me I had nothing to worry about and he was proved to be right – we never had any trouble.

After the initial shock of my appearance in uniform as I went to and from work, there was never a word said against me or my family from the people in Partick. Even the criminals who lived in the area seemed bemused by my presence. They had known me all my life and I had gone to school with many of them and most people just seemed pleased to see a local lad finding a decent job. Later, when I married and we lived in a different street in Partick, both my wife and I were always treated with respect by people living nearby – even by those I later had to arrest!

When my new colleagues and I arrived at the training school in Oxford Street, we were paraded in a small, enclosed courtyard by the inspector and two sergeants. I was shocked to be told that I needed a haircut, as I had had one the previous Saturday. I was to have three haircuts in the next four weeks before my turnout was deemed to be acceptable. In the small, dusty classrooms, we were put through our paces on the rudiments of Scots Law and told what would be expected of us when we joined our shifts.

The City of Glasgow Police operated on three shifts and an officer would work six weeks' continuous night shifts – seven days on and two days off. This was followed by twelve weeks of alternate early and late shifts. Officers on each shift were also allocated a different subgroup to ensure that they were not all off at the same time. So, the people on each shift changed, depending on which subgroup was off.

There was an expectation that no police officer would take unplanned time off, particularly on late shifts and night shifts and especially at weekends. As I was later to discover, it was even difficult to arrange time off for a family wedding or christening. However, the most important lesson that was drummed into me at training school was the importance of upholding the good name of the Force and to act with integrity at all times.

Soon it was time to head down to Albion Street to get kitted out with our uniforms and equipment. The old salts who worked at the store – many former police officers – had heard every excuse in the land to justify extra issues of kit. They were a hardy gang and knew exactly how to deal with such requests and also knew how to cause maximum embarrassment when refusing them. Officers were issued with exactly what it said on the form, nothing more or less. As we had been warned earlier, we had to check the forms we signed to ensure we had all our equipment – if any was missing we would have to pay for it.

The most important thing was to ensure the kit fitted and all the equipment was in working order but just wearing the uniform was a real culture shock. I had to learn how the shirts with their detachable collars worked and the best way to wear my cap.

However, that was some way off as new recruits were told not to wear the uniform until initial training at the Scottish Police College had been completed. There was an understandable fear that a new recruit could become caught up in an incident or be targeted by neds, who might realise that he or she was 'still in cellophane'. I walked out of the stores with a couple of black bags full of gear, but as I was still living at home with my parents in the flat in Partick, I could hardly even find the space to store my gear.

We were naturally keen to get started as soon as possible. Talking with the other newcomers there was an obvious thrill, tempered by a touch of fear, about whether we would prove to be up to the job.

Finally, it was time to head off to the Scottish Police College in Fife which meant we would start to dress in uniform. This also meant yet more haircuts. There seemed very little hair left to cut but, if this was the worst thing to happen to me, I was happy to go along with it. The back of my head started to look like a shaved backside but I understood that I was being tested and needed to measure up.

After all, I was a Glaswegian not a Highlander, I came from a Catholic background and my family had no history of working in the police. Before I was selected, the checks would have shown that my father had been a guest at the Marine police office some years before. The training sergeants had to be confident that I would stay the course.

After passing all the examinations and practical tests at the college, it was time to head back to Oxford Street for a final week's training before being released on the unsuspecting public. I was as fit as I had ever been and had won the long-distance running trophy at the Scottish Police College. Feeling physically strong, I was ready to face the challenges ahead.

8

My First Arrest

During the final week at the Oxford Street training school, the new recruits joined our assigned divisions for an evening on the beat. I was sent to the Northern division, which had its headquarters in Maitland Street, adjacent to Cowcaddens. It was an area I did not know well but I was pleased to be sent to what appeared to be a busy and hard-working office. I was told to report at 7.30pm on Thursday for my first uniform duty.

I had been told that the police office was directly opposite the Cowcaddens subway exit, next to Dallas's department store and as I set off wearing my uniform for the first time I felt uncomfortable and conspicuous. It felt as though everyone would know I was the new boy and would realise I didn't know what I was doing.

I entered the Partick subway for my first free ride. All officers in uniform and detectives, who are given a pass, travelled free on the city transport at that time. As I sat in the nearly empty carriage, I was full of excitement at what lay ahead. In spite of not yet knowing what to do, I felt that, with a bit of luck and some good colleagues, it would all work out for the best.

Arriving at Cowcaddens a few minutes early, I couldn't see the police station and the layout was not as it had been described to me. Worried that I had misunderstood my directions, I looked for someone to ask – but how could I, a policeman in uniform, ask someone where my police station was? Looking for someone in uniform, I saw a local bus inspector. I went over and, admitting I was new to the job, told him I was looking for Maitland Street Police Station.

An older man, extremely well turned out in his green tunic and cap, the inspector walked me behind the department store to a small lane leading to my new office. Rather than enter by the front, the inspector, who I was later to get to know well, led me around the back. He told me that most police officers entered by this back door and I gladly followed his advice.

The back entrance was like an old stable with a few spaces for cars and some box rooms that were the drivers' offices and stores. This led into a dark underground passageway under the foundations of the building and then to some wooden stairs. At the top of the stairs, I opened the door and stumbled out on to the linoleum floor. In front of me, three constables were struggling with a drunken prisoner who was obviously not keen to go to the cells. They all seemed to halt momentarily as I stumbled in but soon continued their struggle, subdued the man and led him away to the cells.

The duty officer, a uniformed inspector who worked at the charge bar, looked at me with a little curiosity. I'm sure that he viewed a new probationer as a chance for some sport but he told me that my colleague for that night, or neighbour in police parlance, was just finishing his piece break and would be down to collect me soon.

I sat waiting on a bench in the corner until, finally, a huge former army man, Alex Adair, came over and told me that I would be heading out with him. Alex had a great reputation, as well as a good sense of humour and I could not have picked a better start to my service. As the two of us set off from the station, we must have looked a funny pair – me just a slim trim 5ft 10in and Alex a massive, big man over 6ft tall.

Alex took me along the Cowcaddens leading towards Buchanan Street and began to explain the beat system to me. He also told me that, although I would be joining his shift for six weeks on nights, my own shift would be on nights for the six weeks after that so I faced a total of twelve weeks on the night shift. I wasn't worried about this and was just looking forward to starting work.

As we walked down Buchanan Street, moving at what appeared to me to be a magisterial pace, Alex led me into a car park explaining that thieves had been targeting it to steal car radios. No sooner had he told me than I heard the sound of breaking glass in the far corner of the car park. In the dim light, I could just see the outline of someone entering a Ford Cortina. Without a second's hesitation, I set off running towards it. Alex, who obviously hadn't heard the breaking glass, followed on once he realised what was happening.

Given his build and years, Alex was never going to move as quickly as his nineteen-year-old probationer. By the time I had reached the car, the thief saw he had been spotted and took off in the opposite direction.

The thief was about my size and build, so I was confident that once I laid my hands on him, I could overpower him. It was March and I had decided to wear my greatcoat, partly because it made me look so smart but it wasn't long before I realised that decision had been a big mistake. In the chase, the coat began to feel incredibly heavy and I was sweating profusely, but that didn't matter because I could see there was nowhere for the thief to go. He was cornered, heading for a low boundary wall and for the first time I was to learn never to try and second guess what a suspect will do. I could only watch as he jumped the wall, using one arm to pole-vault over the side and disappear from view.

When I reached the wall, I looked down to see a drop of some thirty feet and the crumpled form of the thief picking himself up and limping off down Buchanan Street. There was no way I was going back to Alex empty-handed, so I lowered myself as far as I could and then let go. As I hit the tarmac, I quickly realised why the thief had limped away. My ankles and knees were very sore with the sudden jolt.

With my new police cap in my hand and the buttons of my greatcoat now undone, I set off down Buchanan Street, crossed Renfrew Street and headed towards Bath Street. I was about a block behind my suspect, but I thought that he couldn't be as fit as me and would soon be thinking of giving up. As he just kept going, I realised I'd underestimated him.

People stood staring as I gave chase at full pelt. Suddenly I got my second wind. As he fled into Bath Street, I was starting to make ground on him but he continued his run, block after block. Finally, he turned right into North Street and then right again into Sauchiehall Street where I jumped on top of him, just as he was trying to cross the road outside the Locarno dance hall. People who had been standing at a nearby bus stop came to help me but my prisoner, exhausted from the chase, just lay gasping for breath.

Soaked in sweat, I was elated to have caught the thief. I could face my neighbour knowing I had played my part. A few minutes later a police van pulled up and out jumped Alex. In those days, we didn't even have radios, and I had no idea what I should do with my prisoner. Fortunately, someone had phoned in and reported the young officer lying on the pavement with a prisoner in handcuffs.

Very quickly, I realised that Alex was not pleased with me. Once we had the prisoner back in the police office, Alex took me aside. He warned me that, as the senior officer, he was responsible for my safety and, if I was to have a future in the police, I needed to think about my responsibility to others. I shouldn't just rush off without support. I had been lucky that night but, in a big city like Glasgow, I might not be so lucky next time. I took my warning seriously but at the end Big Alex gave me a smile and a pat on the back that left me in no doubt that I had earned his respect. It was a great start to my career.

When I returned home my mother had already left for her night shift at the Southern General but my father had waited up for me. I gave him a blow-by-blow account of my night's work and I could see how much he enjoyed it. He was pleased that his son had made an arrest on his first night as he was amused to learn the prisoner had come from his home part of the city, the Garngad, off Royston Road.

My mother heard the same tale the next morning but, although she was worried about the dangers of the job, she said little about my decision to join the police. Deep down, I knew she was happy and I think somewhat relieved that I had finally found something I really wanted to do.

The following morning, all the probationers were full of stories about our first patrols in the different divisions. Although I'm sure I played it down as best I could, I'm certain I would have been beaming with the pleasure of making my first criminal arrest. I couldn't wait to get back on the streets to see what would happen next.

9

A Hard Day's Night –
Life on the Dawn Patrol

The next Monday night I reported to Maitland Street to really start the job – at least I now knew where to go. The experience of making my first arrest and my knowledge of about half of the beats meant that I was no longer concerned that I wouldn't know what I was doing.

It was time to get down to some hard graft and the process of learning how to do the job. As I left the subway station, I saw my new friend the bus inspector standing at the lights at Dallas's department store and wished him well as I headed into the back door of the police station to start my shift.

When I arrived at the charge bar I was unsure about where to report. When I presented myself to the duty officer, it was clear my reputation had arrived ahead of me. The Inspector gave me clear instructions about what he expected from me during the coming weeks and also made it very plain that he was pleased that I was not going to be a permanent fixture on his shift. The feeling was mutual.

I was sent up to the muster hall where the shift would gather to be briefed before heading out on duty. It was here that we were also expected to write out reports in longhand. These reports were then checked by the sergeants before being sent to the typists.

The muster hall was a wooden office at the back of the

station above the car park. I was told to sit on a bench at the side of the room. The Inspector would brief the eight or nine officers, giving them a defined beat to walk and telling them about any particular issues they needed to know about that day. The officers were then all handed a small list of registration numbers, updated every day, of cars known to be stolen across the city.

That night the Inspector addressed me, telling me what he expected me to do. He also told me to obey instructions from everyone on the shift before sending me out on the beat with a senior constable.

In those dim and distant days, the streets were much quieter at night as the pubs closed at 10pm. During the week, many closed even earlier if business was poor.

The front beats, the busiest ones, were along Sauchiehall Street, including Charing Cross and Georges Cross up to Kelvinbridge. As a rookie, I was sent up to Garscube Road and Mosshouse, an area that was usually quiet on the night shift. As I walked the streets with my new colleague, our conversation covered every conceivable subject. The time between 4.30am and 7am seemed to go very slowly and the discussion helped pass the time.

Our main duty was to patrol the area and provide a presence to help deter housebreakers and thieves. During the second half of the shift, every business premises on the beat was checked, both front and back, to make sure it had not been broken into. Any break-ins missed by the night shift would be the subject of a written report of explanation the following night. As plate-glass windows, fire doors and padlocks all had to be checked, I often found myself scurrying over walls in backcourts and cutting through dunnies or tunnels under tenements to gain access to the back doors. This routine was not for the faint-hearted.

I soon realised that a few of the officers were not very keen on such duties and would just patrol the front areas and send probationers down the back lanes. They often whistled as they patrolled the street fronts in their steel-tipped boots, as they knew there would be less chance of coming face to face with a criminal and a possible violent confrontation.

One night, I was checking the back courts behind a series of semi-derelict shops when I saw a pair of feet sticking out from a shelter behind a building. At first I wasn't convinced that I had really seen a pair of legs so I went nearer to take a closer look. I could see the legs clearly and the body appeared to be naked from the thighs down. It looked as if it was going to be my first dead body. Suddenly, as I stepped closer, all hell broke loose and I got the fright of my life.

Above me, two night shift colleagues lay in wait to ambush me and they threw empty milk bottles down which smashed beside me and the 'victim' as they screamed loudly. They were in hysterics because I was scared out of my wits. My partner, who had been checking around the front, came to see if I was all right. I had been well and truly initiated on to the shift. Other probationers had run away in fear, but they thought I was OK as I had stood my ground. Eventually, I was able to see the funny side and being able to laugh at myself did me no harm in my colleagues' eyes.

The two practical-joking constables had found a mannequin in a derelict shop and put it away to spook various colleagues on the night shift. Although it was made of painted plaster, it looked very realistic when seen by torchlight. It wasn't the first or the last time they had put the mannequin to good use.

My shift was a mix of people from a variety of backgrounds. As was typical in those days, many were Highlanders, some from the islands, or former military types. Others had drifted in and out of various jobs, such as plastering or bricklaying before joining the police. Once they had joined up, most stayed with the service for thirty years.

During the mid-1970s there were recruitment difficulties,

as a large number of officers who had joined up after the Second World War were due to retire. The wages were also poor. I received just £10 per week for my shift work, while most of the prisoners I arrested were earning at least £20.

As is the way in so many workplaces, the curious mix of officers also had a cornucopia of nicknames. Alex Adair was known as 'Bone Crusher' because he was so strong. One time, I saw Alex prove this reputation by holding on to four prisoners in the middle of a gang fight in Cambridge Street – he had two by the head and the other pair in the crook of his arms.

'Parcels' was always carrying a message or parcel for his wife while out on patrol. It was out on such a message, in a Sauchiehall Street bank whilst paying a bill, complete with a parcel under his arm, that he arrested a bank robber who had tried to hold up the bank just as Parcels walked in.

Another called 'Piecebox' came from mining stock; he always wore pit-style boots to work and carried the largest sandwich box ever seen. Along with 'Bungalow' who had 'nothing on top', Piecebox worked hard in Mosshouse, near Saracen, which, at that time, was a very difficult area to police.

Almost everyone had a nickname and they were so widely used it was sometimes difficult to remember their real names. One of the sergeants was called Sergeant Doberman, after a character in the popular comedy show *Sgt Bilko*. In the show, Doberman was small, fat and funny in a stupid kind of way. Our sergeant was very similar. He didn't find it at all amusing when a new constable, believing it was his real name, addressed him as Sergeant Doberman. For weeks afterwards, we all paid the price for this insult.

Doberman's favourite trick was to place a whole steak pie in his mouth in one go, chew it and then swallow. On many a late shift he would sit through in his room lobbing pies into his mouth in this fashion.

A few weeks later, having moved to my own shift, I found myself sent out to patrol on my own because of manpower shortages. Most of the shift usually went out on patrol on their own – they only went with a partner if there was a threat of violence or when checking out a housebreaking. As a probationer, I should have had a tutor constable with me all the time but, when I was sent out alone, I took it as a vote of confidence in me. In hindsight, it was probably just a vote of desperation due to staff shortages.

At this time, contact with the office was kept by using the police boxes positioned along the beats. Officers were expected to keep an eye on the boxes and if the light was on, it meant there had been a call for assistance. If I needed help, I was told to blow my trusty Thunderer whistle, which we were issued with at the stores.

I have to admit that after a long night shift I was often ready to fall asleep in the police box as I waited to meet the sergeant sent out to check on the constable's work. These old police boxes had a small heater and desk and by five or six in the morning it didn't take much to make the eyes close. One morning, I did fall asleep standing inside the box but luckily I heard the sergeant approach just before he opened the box door.

In those first twelve weeks, I had learned so much about the city of Glasgow, how it operated and the people who lived in it. I had attended domestic disputes as well as assaults and break-ins at houses with my colleagues.

On Friday and Saturdays, the night shift started work at 9pm on anti-violence patrols to help the late shift deal with the huge number of reports. On the same evenings, the late shift stayed on until one and two in the morning for the same reasons. Even with this extra manpower there seldom seemed to be enough officers in the sub division.

Gang fights broke out in the city centre at the weekends, as the various groups from the schemes around the city headed into the city for a night in the dance halls or pubs. As if by magic, thirty or forty neds would appear suddenly at a street corner and start slashing and stabbing each other, almost by appointment.

They were so engrossed in kicking and punching each other that they would often not spot the police when we turned up. They seldom missed the arrival of the blue Commer van used by each division. The van was used by the 'Untouchables', a group of plainclothes officers who patrolled each weekend to deal with the violence. As a beat officer, there was no better sight than this van turning into your street to lend a hand.

It was during my initial few weeks as a probationer that I first became aware of the almost mystical 'doss' – a place an officer could go for a cup of tea or a bite to eat out of the elements and away from the public gaze. Every officer guarded his dosses jealously; they were very personal places an officer wouldn't want spoilt by others. There was an unwritten rule that, should a colleague take you into one of his dosses, you wouldn't return alone without his agreement.

In the city, it was easy for beat officers to find a doss among the abundance of pubs, clubs, restaurants and hotels happy to see the local patrol officer and give him a cup of tea or a bowl of soup. Officers like me, pounding the streets around Garscube Road or Mosshouse, had a more difficult time, as there was hardly anything open at night and little chance of a break.

By the end of my first twelve weeks, I thought I had discovered my first doss. I had been out with a few officers during this time but none of them had taken me into a building off North Woodside Road which always had its lights on at night when I passed by. One night, I decided to pay it a visit in the hope of finding somewhere I could call in for a break.

I was on the second half of the night shift and had just finished checking the front and back of a row of shops on Garscube Road near to the junction with North Woodside

Road at the traffic lights. It has since been rebuilt and the site now houses a school. I knocked on the door and waited in the hallway. Soon I could hear someone coming and I was greeted by a friendly man, who seemed surprised but delighted by my unexpected visit. He invited me in for the promised cup of tea.

As we walked through the building towards a double door I became aware of a sweet smell. At first, I was confused as it reminded me of the body sweat and dirt that I recalled from visiting my father in hospital and there seemed to be a lot of heat in the air. As my host opened the double door, I saw a sight that shocked me to my very core. I had called at a model lodging house for homeless men run by the council – a genuine doss house.

I had never seen anything like it despite my years living in Glasgow. It was like a scene from a Charles Dickens novel. There were around one hundred men in a large room. In the dim light, I could make out that they were in various states of drunkenness. Some were staggering around, others were just merry and some morose and immobile. In the centre of the room was a thirty-foot long black-leaded oven and grill arrangement which many of the men were using to cook on. It made the room extremely hot and the strong, sweet stench was overpowering.

As I desperately tried to avoid retching, I was aware of the men staring at me, wondering why I had invaded their world when there was no trouble for me to sort out. My host led me to a small anteroom adjacent to the cooking area with just a perspex window between the room and the men.

There was no way I could drink tea in there, no matter the man's kindness. With the stench of the place, I knew I could not hold it down. I thanked him, promised that I would return another time and, after being shown more of the building, I left as soon as I could.

It seemed unbelievable that human beings had to live in

such circumstances. These men, many of whom were working in low-paid jobs, had to queue to get a pot to cook their meals or make a cup of tea. They had no privacy and, for the most part, seemed to ignore each other's presence.

Their bedrooms, I discovered, consisted of a caged area with room for just a single bed and bedside cupboard, with no toilet or bathing facilities, other than communal services at the end of the corridor. Every man had to keep his possessions with him at all times, as they were likely to be stolen. It was an awful place and one that I visited only when I had to, usually when a resident died, which was mostly from an alcohol-related illness.

Meanwhile, back at the police office, I was still only allowed to sit on the side bench kept for the probationers. It was some time later, though I don't know what I had done to deserve the change in status, before I was invited to join the teatime card school that meant I could sit with the rest of the men on the shift.

There was no better feeling than heading home after a night shift: tired, ready for bed but seeing everyone else heading off in the wind and the rain for their day's work.

A run home on the subway, a breakfast of fresh hot rolls from the bakery and a read of the newspaper were the perfect end to a night shift. I would then snuggle up for good day's sleep and it wasn't unusual for me to sleep in and not get out of bed until after 6pm.

At one stage, I was moved to Roystonhill to walk the beat there. On the hill, Esther's chip shop sat in the centre of a row of dilapidated tenement buildings. Due to the pending redevelopment, the area was badly neglected and, as a result, the target for thieves. On the night shift, I used to wait in the darkness of the derelict buildings and catch the occasional housebreaker as they tried to break into the shops.

Esther was a kind-natured woman, who used to ensure

that, at the end of each night, there was a bag of chips left over for the beat man. Once she had got to know me and realised what I was doing, she tried to persuade me not to take chances during the night. She thought the break-ins were not important enough to risk personal injury. Like many of the beat officers in the area, I was grateful for Esther's concerns but this was the job I had chosen to do. For Esther's part, she always left me a nice fish supper and a bottle of juice. There was no better luxury on a night shift as I waited for the thieves to come out.

10
Having a Gas –
the Quick Route to CID

By the summer of 1971 Frankie Vaughan had sung and danced his way into the hearts of the Glasgow neds. Frankie had managed to bring peace between rival gangs in Easterhouse, if you could believe the press. At police stations dustbins piled high with knives and machetes were displayed openly and the media had had a field day claiming Frankie had finally brought peace to the city.

So it was something of surprise when I turned up for my first night shift in Easterhouse to be met on the streets by groups of teenagers and men armed with sticks, bottles, knives and machetes. Along with the rest of my shift, I had been transferred to this notorious scheme on the outskirts of Glasgow. No doubt these gangs were just visitors to the scheme playing war games!

Although the Frankie Vaughan initiative was well intentioned, it soon became clear that not much had changed. The one lasting improvement was the creation of an innovative Easterhouse project, a youth club to take teenagers off the streets and give them something to keep them away from the gangs. There was no doubt that the project, based in Nissen-style huts off Lochdochart Road, was extremely worthwhile but to police officers it just seemed like another set of huts for gangs of local neds to meet in. However, as long they didn't interfere with us, we left them alone.

As the heat of the summer grew, so did the number of gang disorders. On the late and night shifts our Pye police radios repeatedly crackled into life with a 'Code 23' – the code for gang fight or 'group disorder' as it was poetically titled.

Once the Code 23 came in we would set off, usually on our own, as fast as our 1000cc Morris vans would allow us. In those days, police officers were sent out with just an eighteen-inch-long wooden baton to take on the gangs. So we very keen to make sure exactly where each of our colleagues were, in case any of us got into serious difficulties.

Having accepted the Code 23 I would drive as quickly as possible with the headlights on, engine screaming in low gear but at high speed (relatively speaking) and with the wheels spinning. Usually this was enough to persuade the would-be gladiators to do a runner and realising their fun was over, they would rush to a nearby house to dump their weapons. There were occasions though when some warrior had taken his brave pills – usually too much fortified wine – and decided to take on the police. Without the protection of today's police officer, you were expected to challenge the ned, dressed in just shirtsleeves and armed with only a baton. There were nights when you had to be careful. Somehow you soon got a nose for when trouble was brewing; you could sense the electricity in the air. Different things seemed to set it off: a major Old Firm game, the weather was too hot, there was no rain, or even a full moon.

My colleagues and I began to weary of this regular Code 23 engagement and we started to get concerned about our safety. There was no option other than to turn up and face up to the mob. If you failed, the neds knew you were scared and would take advantage of you in the future. There was no doubt that some officers took a little longer to arrive at the scene than others and there was a real fear that one of us was going to end up badly injured.

With just six officers at most lining up for a shift to cover Easterhouse the tensions in the muster hall soon came to the surface. It was the height of the Troubles in Northern Ireland and every day we would see pictures of our colleagues in the RUC taking on similar mobs backed by the Army and armed with gas and shields. To us, our wooden batons were not fit for purpose.

Our redoubtable sergeant, Harry Orr, had to maintain peace on the shift and could always be relied for support. By the end of the summer he had had enough of us moaning. One Friday late shift in September we turned up for duty to be told that the Chief Constable had finally recognised our plight and we were to be issued with CS gas grenades. These grenades were to be held at Easterhouse but the launcher was to be kept five miles away in divisional HQ. We were told that this was to ensure that the Shift Inspector would always be involved in the decision to deploy the gas and thus allow a cooling-off period before the gas was actually used on the streets.

We constables were unhappy with this arrangement but were glad our plight was finally being recognised. We were all issued with gas masks and had great time fooling about wearing them. We also had to ponder such difficult problems as whether to wear our hats with our gas masks. At muster that Friday late shift, the Chief Constable's order was read out – we were ready for action. Not quite all of us though. One constable, Hughie Mould, turned up late, as usual, for the muster only to find there wasn't a gas mask for him. Hughie was so unhappy he phoned the supplies department back in Glasgow to complain bitterly at the lack of gas masks in Easterhouse. The supply officer was bemused by Hughie's request but, as always in the police force, thought he was merely 'out the loop' and promised to resolve the matter. Satisfied that he had wreaked havoc with HQ, Hughie then started his late shift manning the office. At five o'clock in the afternoon all the late shift at Barlanark sub-station were suddenly ordered to return to the office immediately.

Given the unusual transmission we all rushed back thinking something very important was about to occur . . . and it was. I arrived back at the police caravan that passed for Barlanark police office and I saw the Chief Superintendent's car parked at the front. As the shift lined up in the muster hall the duty superintendent began to read the Riot Act about the use of CS gas in Easterhouse. We didn't know what to make of it.

It quickly became clear that HQ had no idea we were to use the gas and they wanted to know all about it. This particular superintendent wasn't famous for his understanding nature and milk of human kindness. We were all shocked when our sergeant stepped forward to accept the blame. It turned out there had been no CS gas, no launcher for the grenade and no Chief Constable's order.

The sergeant admitted that he had found the gas masks on a council tip and had brought them to the office as a joke to cheer up the shift. Without Hughie Mould's phone call to supplies it would have remained just that – a laugh.

Unfortunately it became much more as HQ believed that we had declared war on the population of Easterhouse. Poor Harry Orr not only received a severe reprimand from the Superintendent but also had to face a weekend of constant wind-ups from the shift about the gas masks. The episode did cheer us up but we still had to take on the local neds, who did not always abide by the rules of engagement, armed with just our batons.

One such group was led by the Logue family – father, son and friends who rioted regularly in the streets, damaging local cars and houses. One Saturday evening I and several other officers arrived at their street to find the entire family out on the road armed with samurai swords. They were attacking their neighbours who had evidently had enough of the nonsense. The Logues and their associates had started fighting rival gangs early that evening but had run out of opposition. High on alcohol, the gang had returned to their street and had begun to damage their neighbours' cars. Quite rightly the neighbours were outraged and, after ringing for the police, went out on to the street in an attempt to stop the damage.

Many of these neighbours were big, hard-working men who just wanted some peace and quiet at the weekend after a week's hard slog. They had had enough of the Logues and when we arrived there was utter mayhem with twenty thugs running on the street waving sticks, knives and swords. A similar number of local men and women were trying to protect themselves and their property from attack. We joined in the melee and the four of us managed to arrest and cuff half a dozen of the key players, including the Logues. By the end of the weekend, the whole family was locked up for mobbing, rioting and associated charges. A range of weapons, bloodstained clothing and photographs of witnesses' injuries had been collected along with dozens of statements. Peace had eventually been restored, if only for a brief period, to a small part of what was then the biggest housing estate in Europe.

These experiences were exactly what an ambitious young officer like me wanted. I had come to see how detective officers worked on the numerous serious assaults and housebreakings we reported and at this time, was ambitious to join the CID and become a detective. I started to know the local criminals and became well known to them across Easterhouse, Barlanark, Garthamlock and Ruchazie. I also began to develop informants in these schemes and my sergeants would let me work on after the end of a shift if

I had enquiries to make. They also made sure other shift supervisors would help me.

On one occasion I heard about a group of teenage housebreakers from the Torran Road area of Easterhouse. They were breaking into houses all over the scheme every day and, armed with their names and addresses and information about their stolen goods, I presented myself at the CID office ready for action. My reception was not what I had anticipated. Far from being impressed, the detective, who was far too busy to take much interest, told me just to get on with it. He did, however, arrange for a warrant which would allow us to search the houses I'd identified.

Within a couple of hours, armed with my Justice of the Peace warrant, I set off with several colleagues to search the houses. The first house was in Torran Road and at that time it was a hostile area for the police. The house was a three-storey terraced property with five bedrooms built to cope with the large families then prevalent in the area. I was not greeted warmly when I turned up on the doorstep with the warrant. The harassed mother of the house needed me turning up like she needed a sore head. She said that she had no idea who was in the house or the whereabouts of her sons, who were the targets of the first part of my enquiry. She could not and would not help me, so there was nothing else for it but to search the entire house.

I can still vividly recall the foul stench in the house – a mixture of animals, urine and the stale odour of food and alcohol from the previous night. The multicoloured carpets hid a thousand secrets and the sticky mess left our boots in a terrible state. Mountains of discarded dirty clothes were left on every floor as if some magical intervention would get them washed.

There seemed to be dozens of adults and children running around the house who all started panicking as we started our search. Usually such raids were carried out by senior CID detectives and our suspects clearly felt cheated by being turned over by a bunch of rookies.

After a long search we managed to recover the stolen goods I had been told were there. This raid led us to a further four houses and in all we arrested five housebreakers and recovered televisions, jewellery, toasters and many other things stolen from the local area.

I was ecstatic but in the subdivision many regarded it as just another 'turn'. Despite this lack of recognition, I was extremely pleased and, with the help of the local detectives, was able to write up my custody case for the next morning's court. I had made my mark and it was noticed. It was now time for me to move to the Criminal Investigation Department.

The CID officers were happy to have me seconded to them as an aide for a few months because of my local knowledge of the neds and my experience of the serious assaults, disorders and the car thieves working in the area. I had eighteen months' service under my belt and I felt that I'd arrived. The world seemed a great place.

Within months, I was interviewed for a vacancy in the Criminal Investigation Department. In spite of my youth and my relative inexperience, I was successful and became a detective constable in the Northern Division. No sooner had I found my feet than I was transferred to CID Headquarters to join the Drugs Squad – the only one in Scotland at the time. A year later, I was transferred again to the newly formed Serious Crime Squad and began to build on the knowledge and experience colleagues had shared with me.

11
Carstairs – Catching up with Scotland's Most Notorious Killer

For those of us in the Serious Crime Squad, the final week of November 1976 started out like any other. I was sent to East Kilbride as part of a team of officers to help with a sexual assault investigation and such duties were amongst the least popular. They took us away from our usual investigations and the local detectives did not welcome the invasion by outsiders. However, it was essential that the squad showed its worth to the divisions otherwise we could not expect their support in the future.

East Kilbride was a cold and miserable place to work in the winter. We began the long slog of door-to-door inquiries. This can be a frustrating and boring job but it is essential to focus on the answers being given on the doorstep. They often hold the key to solving such crimes. It is all the more challenging when it's obvious that most people have little or no interest in your questions and are very keen to see the young detective head back down the drive and leave them in peace. By teatime on the second day I was getting frustrated as not a single squad officer had yet found a significant lead. However, as we met at East Kilbride police office after our meal, ready to head back out to pound the streets yet again, a rumour started to circulate that there had been some kind of incident at Carstairs Mental Hospital as it was called then. At first it wasn't clear what had happened but soon there were rumours there had been some sort of breakout.

From the outside, Carstairs Hospital looked very much like a prison but it was notorious as an asylum for the criminally insane. Built on either side of the main road through the village, the hospital clung to a hillside with each building surrounded by high-security fences. It was an unwelcoming, bleak place, open and exposed to the elements. Among these buildings were a number of high-security wards which contained the most dangerous inmates, amongst whom were some of the most notorious criminals in Scotland. A year earlier I had visited Carstairs as part of an initial training course for detectives; the day was to help us understand the particular problems of dealing with the criminally insane. I vividly recall that day. I had set off by bus with the twenty colleagues on the course and a handful of instructors. En route, we were a typical jocular bunch of young police officers excited by our day out together. By the end of it, there was no such humour. The reality of life at Carstairs and the obvious dangers faced by the dedicated staff working behind the high-security fences had shaken even the hardiest and most cynical young officers. The evening trip back to Glasgow had been in silence as we all contemplated what we had seen.

That day's visit was at the forefront of my mind as rumours of the outbreak circulated the police station. Whilst East Kilbride was cold and unwelcoming at that time of year, Carstairs was far worse, located in the middle of nowhere in deepest Lanarkshire. It was a remote place with just a few isolated houses and a difficult place to find your way around on a dark winter's night. Around 7pm it became clear that not only had there been a breakout, there had also been people murdered at the hospital. The full picture was still not clear but there was a rumour that a patient and one of the nursing staff had been murdered.

When it became apparent that the escapees had overpowered a police officer and had managed to get hold of a car, I and three other detectives set off for Hamilton police office to collect some firearms. We each carried personal issue firearms authorisation cards to allow us to be issued with .38 Smith & Wesson handguns without delay. However, the Duty Inspector had other ideas. He said that he didn't have the authority to issue firearms to a group of detectives from Glasgow who were on duty in Lanarkshire. Strathclyde Police had just come into being in 1975 and there were a range of administrative processes yet to be agreed – the issue of firearms to the Serious Crime Squad being one of them. Despite being on the hunt for an escaped killer we could not draw the weapons we needed to go and tackle him. So the four of us were forced to race back to Tobago Street police office in Glasgow where we could legally be issued with firearms. It was a return journey of fourteen miles but we knew it was the quickest way to resolve our crisis. It would not be the only time in my career that bureaucracy was to delay police operations.

By the time we had been issued with our pistols in Glasgow and began the journey back to Lanarkshire, the police radio messages were telling us that the suspects had stolen not only a police car but had then broken into a house and stolen the owner's car.

The suspects were thought to be heading south down the A74 towards Carlisle and we were now on the same road about twenty miles behind. Our car, a yellow Mark 3 Cortina, was the worst vehicle in our fleet. The headlights didn't work properly, pointing almost directly down on to the roadway in front of the car, the brakes were tentative to say the least and it was freezing as the heater wasn't working. The car was due to be scrapped in the coming weeks. It was fine for door-to-door enquiries but it wasn't the car to pursue dangerous killers on the run from Carstairs. Nevertheless, it soon became clear that we were the best-placed officers to lead the chase.

The tension was palpable from the radio messages passing back and forth between Carstairs and police headquarters. We could hear the sense of urgency in the dispatchers' voices, usually so calm, yet verging on the excited. Suddenly, we were asked to change frequency to a talk-through on Channel 5 and Chief Constable David McNee addressed the four of us. He told us that two Carstairs patients had escaped and had killed at least three people. They were deemed to be extremely dangerous. He told us that it was our duty to take all steps possible to prevent any further danger to the public.

So there we were, four experienced police officers, each armed with a revolver and twelve rounds of ammunition, racing down the A74 in a car fit only to be scrapped. In those days of primitive communications, once we were past Lesmahagow we no longer had any link to the outside world. Just before then we had been told that one of our police colleagues had also been murdered by the people we were now hunting.

It began to snow as we skidded and slid south into the darkness in a car with a useless set of headlights. Suddenly, on an off-ramp in front of us we saw headlights and the rotating blue lights of various police cars. We left the A74 expecting to find a stand-off between the suspects and the local police officers but instead discovered that our escapers had driven to the roundabout, stopped their vehicle, calmly got out of their car and laid down in the roadway to give themselves up. We arrived just as the prisoners were being taken to Carlisle police office.

Within the hour it had been decided that we would be responsible for returning our suspects to Scotland immediately. I recall clearly the ancient stone cell block at the police office where I witnessed Robert Mone and Thomas McCulloch being charged in connection with the escape and subsequent murders of that night. I remember taking Mone to a second police car that had subsequently arrived at Carlisle and with a colleague I sat in the rear of the car with a handcuffed killer. Mone had been sent to Carstairs for one of the most appalling crimes ever committed in Scotland. At the age of nineteen he had shot dead a pregnant Dundee schoolteacher, Nanette Hanson, in front her class of fourteen-year-olds. Now, along with McCulloch, he had killed again, just a few hours before. The atmosphere at Carlisle police office and later that night at Lanark police office was electric. There were dozens of uniformed police officers all keen to play their part in the arrest of those responsible for the Carstairs murders, particularly as one of our own was a victim.

Heading back up the A74, I was keen to understand Mone and McCulloch as best I could. Mone presented himself as a scrawny, sinewy individual who seemed too slight to have been involved in the mayhem of that night. McCulloch seemed no better but he clearly played second fiddle to Mone. What struck me most clearly about Mone, though, was his complete lack of anxiety and stress. He appeared calm and in full control yet only a few hours earlier he had killed PC George Taylor with an axe. Mone showed no signs of worry or indeed remorse. In fact he seemed to be entertained by the huge circus around him as we brought him and McCulloch back to Scotland.

As we headed north I pointed out to Mone that it would not be long before he would be back in Carstairs Hospital again. His response surprised me. Mone explained quietly that he knew he would not be returning to that institution ever again. When I asked him to explain, given the murder that night of three innocent people surely proved that he was mentally ill, Mone answered that the authorities could not afford to let him or McCulloch return to Carstairs. If the pair were returned to the mental asylum and something were to happen to either of them then all hell would break loose politically. The sole reason for his escape was so that he could not be returned to Carstairs but instead be treated as a bona fide prisoner and serve his time in a jail. His reasoning was that if he could serve his time in a prison, he would have to be given a date for release. He insisted that, as a patient at Carstairs, he could not depend on a release date at any time.

I found his logic incredible and left Mone in no doubt about my own thoughts but that did not shake him at all. He merely invited me to wait and see who would be proved right. Mone then went on to tell me how he and McCulloch had planned each detail of the escape for months. They had prepared knives, ropes and even identity cards for use once outside the hospital. Mone showed obvious delight in how he had duped staff at Carstairs who had thought that the two patients were benefiting from the occupational therapy offered to them. He also realised that his new-found fame would be the subject of a great deal of interest and he gave me a photograph of himself and told me to keep it as a memento of our meeting. The picture was one of a series that Mone had used to create the rudimentary identity cards that we had recovered from him when we searched him in Carlisle. I found his obvious composure shocking. He had no empathy with his victims and showed no regret.

Mone saw the events of that night, including the horrific murders of three innocent people, as entirely necessary to deliver his plan. He insisted that he did not believe that he and McCulloch could evade capture for very long but had been confident that they could both make Carlisle safely before surrendering to the English police. Mone admitted that he feared such an outcome was unlikely had they been intercepted en route by Scottish police officers; he believed that he would have been killed had he been caught on the road in the middle of nowhere. He thought that the killing of a police officer, though unplanned, would have resulted in Scottish colleagues responding in a similar fashion. Although I told him that he would have been safe so long as he offered no threat to arresting police officers no matter where he had been arrested, he was completely unconvinced.

As we returned to Lanark police office in the early hours of 1 December, the approach to the yard was mobbed by camera crews and reporters trying desperately to get a glimpse of Mone and McCulloch. It was still dark and it was a night that seemed to go on and on. As we entered the parking area I put a coat over Mone's head. He still appears to own the sheepskin coat and was pictured wearing it while on day release from prison a couple of years ago. Then I had to take him through the throng of uniformed and plainclothes police officers milling about the rear doors leading to the custody area. I can still recall the grim faces of all these officers, many of whom were close colleagues of the murdered PC George Taylor.

It was around 5am when Mone was finally locked in his cell at Lanark, ending a momentous day that had left a well-regarded nurse, Neil McLellan, forty-six; a Carstairs patient, Iain Simpson, forty; and my twenty-seven-year-old colleague, George Taylor, all murdered. It had been a long day for the four of us involved in the chase but we felt very satisfied to have done our duty. Above all, though, we were tired. Somehow being so close to such evil had exhausted us. It was only now, once we had the pair returned to Lanark and safely in the cells, that we were told the full terrible details of that day's murderous attacks.

Mone and McCulloch had pretended for months to be model prisoners as they hatched their plans to escape. In preparation they had not only created identity cards complete with photographs, they had also constructed a much-needed rope ladder to scale the perimeter fence for an escape. Their nurse, Mr McLellan, worked with them and Iain Simpson in a side room which gave Mone and McCulloch the opportunity to overpower both men by blinding them with paint stripper. The escapers needed Mr McLellan's keys to ensure they could leave the secure building unseen. Unfortunately for their victims they had also decided that neither man could survive for fear that the alarm would be raised prematurely. As a result, both men were mercilessly hacked to death in what must have been a most horrific attack.

Once free, the men had scaled the fence of the hospital under cover of darkness and when they got out onto a nearby road they pretended that one of them was a road accident victim and flagged down a passing car for help. The first car to pass was a police car and Constable Taylor and his colleague stopped and got out to help the apparently injured man. Then, without warning, George Taylor was overpowered and murdered whilst his fellow officer was forced to flee into the nearby fields to escape a similar fate. Mone had carefully avoided telling us these details in his clinical, analytical account of the day.

In 1977, Mone and McCulloch appeared at Edinburgh High Court and pled guilty to the murders. Mone admitted axing to death PC George Taylor and the judge recommended he spend the rest of his life behind bars. As Mone had predicted, neither prisoner was returned to Carstairs but they were sentenced to life imprisonment to be served in the Scottish penal system.

Both prisoners have remained notorious to this day and there is no doubt that they were feared by mainstream criminals who have shared prison landings with them. Over the years, I have often thought of my car journey with Mone and how he predicted the outcome. Changes in human rights legislation mean that, being in prison rather than Carstairs, there is a strong possibility that the two men could now be freed at some time in the near future. Recently Mone was

77

released from prison on accompanied visits to public places. I find it difficult to comprehend the scale of change that Mone needs to face to prepare him for such a day and I hope that the professionals involved truly understand the implications of freeing Mone and McCulloch.

Not long after the events of that terrible night, I tried to speak with George Taylor's family. I wanted to share with them anything that might have helped them understand how their loved one was so unfairly taken from them but I was told that I could not speak to the family as they were too grief-stricken. In the intervening years I again offered to speak with the family but was refused repeatedly and told it was inappropriate. Almost thirty years later I finally met Mrs Taylor and her family. The meeting was arranged with the help of Jimmy McNulty, a retired police officer who helped create an organisation which supports those affected by the death of a serving police officer. I met them at the Scottish Police College during the memorial service for fallen officers. It was the first such service Mrs Taylor had felt able to attend. I talked with the family for a short time but I felt better for being able to share with her the impact that her husband's death had had on a host of people she didn't know and had never met. I think we all felt better for meeting but I wished it could have taken place much sooner.

12

Arthur Thompson and the Strange Case of the Stolen Silver

There are times when policing can be frustrating when the wrong information is received or the intelligence isn't enough to lead to an arrest or conviction. This happened in a case involving the late Arthur Thompson. In the early 1970s Thompson had built up a fearsome reputation as the crime boss of Glasgow. His name often featured in local newspaper reports where he was euphemistically described as a 'well-known colourful Glasgow businessman'. But few doubted his involvement in a whole range of crime as he extorted, assaulted and otherwise intimidated criminals across the city.

I met Arthur Thompson on just a handful of occasions. Once, when I was still a probationer, I had stopped a large luxury car in Garnethill which was going the wrong way down a street. The driver was on his own and, being a keen young probationer, I wanted to impress my older colleague and make sure I went through all the steps correctly. It was only later, at the end of the shift, someone told me I had booked Arthur Thompson – but at the time I didn't even know who he was.

A week later, I was out with my senior police colleague

when we called at an unlicensed club where there had been reports of fighting a few days earlier. When we turned up, the manager offered us a 'refreshment' but, despite refusing his offer, a soft drink appeared in front of me. The manager pointed to Thompson who had sent it over, having recognised me from our earlier meeting.

It was many years later, in January 1977 as a detective in the Serious Crime Squad, that I next came across Arthur Thompson and in the strangest of circumstances. It started when an informant told me that there was some silverware circulating in the East End of Glasgow. The details were vague but it appeared to have come from a housebreaking two years earlier. While the rest of the stolen goods had been sold on, this silver had a heraldic engraving. The thieves were going to melt it all down for its limited precious metal value. The informant wondered if there was any way of saving the silver, which could be historically important.

Arthur Thompson had been approached about the silver by a publican from London Road, in the Calton, to find out if he could get rid of it. This lead was a chance for the squad to get some vital evidence against Thompson, or at least learn how he went about his business. I suggested my informant tell the men he had a potential buyer and say that, if the price was right, the silver would be shipped abroad to either America or Australia.

The next day, I was told the deal had been done. The informant would act as go-between and I could bid for the goods. As I knew the thieves were in a hurry to unload the goods, I was keen to get my hands on the silver to save it from destruction. I needed to try to identify the stolen silver, so it was agreed that I would be given one piece from the set 'so I could be assured of its quality' before I parted with the cash.

That night at 11 o'clock, my informant rang and told me to turn up at a deserted shop in London Road in an hour and a half to collect my sample. With so little time, I had no choice. If I failed to show up then the silver would be heading for the smelter. There was a chance I would be recognised but it was a chance I had to take. As a member of the Serious Crime Squad, I was regularly changing my appearance and street clothes and, at that time, I had hair far longer than was usual for a police officer. I rang my colleagues at the squad to let them know what I was going to do and, accompanied by my informant, I set off for the half past midnight meeting.

The streets of the East End were deserted as we made our way to the London Road meeting, not far from the Barras. My informant was very nervous and so was I, but I didn't want to let on.

It was eerily quiet as I parked the car in St Andrew's Square. The echo of the door closing and our feet on the pavements just added to our tension. The derelict shop was full of heaps of old clothes and debris abandoned by homeless people with the terrible stench of stale life that accompanies it. Outside, my informant waited nervously, fearing what would happen if he was identified with me.

It was soon apparent that we had been watched arriving and there was the noise of a shop shutter opening and closing. Outside, I could hear footsteps and someone speaking to my informant. Suddenly Arthur Thompson stepped into the derelict shop and pulled a large object wrapped in plastic bags from his coat pocket. It turned out to be a large soup ladle. Thompson told me I had to make my mind up about the deal very quickly and, as suddenly as he appeared, he was gone.

By this time, my informant was white with anxiety as Thompson headed off towards the Barras. I was confident that Thompson had not recognised me but I also knew I could not move against Thompson without exposing my informant. I hoped, though, that successful negotiations over the silverware would allow us to take on Thompson in the future.

When I had the chance to examine the ladle, with its engraved handle, I couldn't make any sense of the scrolls. Thompson had given me just a couple of days to decide whether I wanted the silver, otherwise it was all going to be melted down.

The next morning at the Serious Crime Squad's office in Temple police station, I showed off my antique and started trying to trace where it had been stolen from. The boss, John Blincow, was delighted and was keen to make progress. He wanted Thompson's involvement 'kept tight' as it would give us an opportunity to move against him later.

He also wanted a quick identification of the stolen silver so, along with a colleague, I headed off to the office of the Court of Lord Lyon in Edinburgh, which is responsible for all Scottish heraldry. On arrival and somewhat snootily, I was told the ladle was in fact a soup divider but it was identified very quickly as belonging to a family who had stately homes in the West Coast of Scotland as well as London.

Back in Glasgow, I compared the family name I had been given with our crime report records and soon discovered that the divider was owned by Captain Sir Arthur Scott, a distant relative of Sir Walter Scott, who had a house called Glenoris on Mull. There had been a break-in at Glenoris in August 1975 and the silver had been missing since then. The Scott family confirmed the identity of the heraldic scroll and the silver's historical importance.

They also put me in contact with McTear's & Co., a well-known firm of Glasgow auctioneers, who in turn put me in touch with the insurance company who had borne the loss of the original break-in. Without mentioning Arthur Thompson's involvement, I explained the situation and the likelihood that the silver would be lost forever and melted down if I was unable to buy it. A Mr Kirkwood, acting for the insurers, said they would pay £500, and despite this being less than the scrap metal value, he refused to increase the amount. He also said it would take several days to authorise and issue the money.

Later that day, my informant arranged the handover after Thompson had made contact again. Neither of us was very keen to meet up with the criminals again. Although I did not have the cash, my contact said he was prepared to provide the money and I could reimburse him later. Once again he was contacted at short notice and told to return to the London Road shop to collect the silverware. He was told to get rid of the silver and then go to a pub where he was to hand the publican £600 in cash.

We tried, unsuccessfully, to drive the price down to £500 but I thought I could approach police headquarters for the remaining £100. The deal done, 167 silver forks, knives, spoons, tongs, tea strainers, and soup and fish dividers were recovered, all in pristine condition. Although I would have preferred to round up and arrest the key players, at least it was a result for the Scott family and I had by now also identified the housebreakers involved in the original crime.

The next day, I reported the recovery back to the insurers. For some reason, a couple of days later, the goods were then handed over without any cash being exchanged. I was told by John Blincow that the matter was now closed. I was furious. An informant had gone out a limb to help the police and paid £600 out of his own pocket to recover the silver.

John Blincow was a large bluff man, who could be extremely bullish but he was apologetic and very supportive of me on this occasion. He said that because of some unexplained reason which had been decided at headquarters, a policy decision had been made that we could not be involved in this exchange. There had been a lot of publicity about fraudulent transactions involving English police officers engaged in similar recoveries. No one had thought to tell me before the handover had been agreed and, as a relatively junior detective, my views held little sway. My informant was able to tell me the identity of the two men who carried out the original break-in, but given the circumstances, there was little I could do. Nevertheless, over the next two years, they were both arrested and the team, who had travelled around Scotland breaking into rural stately homes, was disbanded.

I was upfront with my informant, telling him the insurance company were not going to reimburse his cash. Needless to say, he was not happy. I promised, though, I would find some way to repay him. My word was enough to allow our relationship to continue. To me, it was very important that I did not take advantage of him and double cross him. He understood my problem and, over the next few years, continued to pass on valuable information.

Mr Kirkwood had the silver and, as far as the parties were concerned, that was an end to the matter. The £600 paid out by the informant remained a sore point for me as I knew he could ill afford to lose the cash. Having discussed the situation with my wife, I decided I should save up and pay him back the money myself.

It those days, £600 was a very large sum of money to me but, within a year or so, I had managed to save it up. One Friday night, I rang the informant and told him to meet me in a pub. At 5.30pm, I took part in a strange ceremony, handing over the cash in a brown envelope. This was the only time that I ever gave money to an informant in all my police service. Initially, he was confused as he had not been expecting the handover. However, once he understood where the cash had come from, he was happy with the resolution.

Whatever the rights and wrongs, I had maintained the integrity of our relationship and had kept my word. I still have the official receipt from McTear's for the silverware which I kept to remind me of my costly decision.

I never had any further dealings with Arthur Thompson and we were never able to link him to the housebreakers.

His involvement with the silver appeared to be because he knew where to get it smelted, for which he would have been paid a fee. I continued to hear rumours about Thompson during the rest of my career. I'm sure he went to his grave without realising that he had handed over stolen silver to a serving police officer who ended up paying for it out of his own pocket!

I have never regretted my decision in the years since. My word was my bond and I felt I had to resolve this matter properly. My informant remained a valuable asset to me for many years, I'm sure partly because of how this difficult situation was resolved.

This wasn't the last that I heard of the silverware. In the 1980s, I was contacted by the Metropolitan Police who wanted to discuss some stolen silver. The family, having decided it was too risky to leave the silverware in their country home, had kept it at their London property. It had been stolen yet again. During the Met enquiry, the family explained how a Glasgow detective had managed to trace the silver and might be able to do so again. There was obviously no link between Glasgow and the London break-in and I certainly wasn't about to repeat my costly mistake. You can imagine my response to my English colleague.

13
Rich and Infamous – the New Brand of Robbers

During 1976 and 1977, there was an unprecedented number of armed robberies at post offices, banks and hospitals across the West of Scotland. They were carried out by a group of violent men who were prepared to shoot, assault and threaten ordinary people going about their everyday business. Whilst some of these robberies appeared to be one-off attempts, there was also a more sinister sequence of robberies planned and executed in a professional fashion. They were carried out by a newly formed gang of career criminals hell bent on becoming rich and famous. One day they would be infamous and imprisoned but, in the interim, they enjoyed a taste of the high life.

On a typically dreich October day in 1976, two masked men, armed with a pistol, burst through the doors of the Glasgow Savings Bank in Station Road, Milngavie. The pistol was held at the face of one of the female members of staff as the men forced the tellers to gather up the cash and put it in a bag they had brought with them. In seconds, the lives of half a dozen people were devastated as the robbers made off in a stolen car with £2,931 – a very impressive sum back in 1976.

On 3 December, the same gang, with some new recruits, stepped up a league and broke into the wages office at

Leverndale Hospital, Crookston, in Glasgow. With military precision, they forced their way into the wages office and, armed with a pistol and a wooden cosh, threatened the three women and two men working there. Less than five minutes later they were heading off in yet another stolen car with more than £17,000 in cash.

Emboldened by their success, the gang ventured out yet again on 25 March 1977. Organised in their typically efficient style, and armed with a sawn-off shotgun and wooden coshes, they raided the wages offices within the grounds of Ruchill Hospital in Glasgow at 9am. Unseen, they crept into the wages section and then forced their way into the clearing office and the weekly pay section. Screaming and swearing, at least three masked robbers crashed through the office door where three female clerks were handling the day's cash.

The gang showed their contempt for their victims by firing the shotgun as a warning and blowing a large hole in the office door. Some distance away, other masked raiders had forced two female switchboard operators to lie on their office floor to prevent the police being called. Within minutes this ruthless and irresponsible gang had fled in stolen cars with just £390.27 and seven cheques which they wouldn't be able to cash. This was going to be my introduction to the gang's activities and one of the most intensive operational periods of my police career.

Responding to the police radio appeal for help, I arrived at Ruchill Hospital to see the effects of the vicious and ruthless raid. In every corner of the office there seemed to be women crying and there were papers strewn all over the floor. To me the shotgun blast through the door felt as if it were a challenge to the police – a challenge I, for one, was happy and ready to accept. Although such a crime was the business of Saracen CID, they were only too grateful for help from the Serious Crime Squad. I started taking statements and trying to build up a sequence of events. A lot of water was to pass under the bridge before we finally caught up with this gang and they had plenty more tricks up their sleeves.

On 27 May, the Clydesdale Bank in High Street, Johnstone, was to be their next target. The masked gang threatened staff and customers with a sword, a hammer and a knife. Cursing and shouting, they then smashed the glass screen in the banking hall and broke desks and office equipment before forcing staff to empty £6,120 in cash into a getaway bag. Once again they set off in a stolen car. The local police arrived shortly after the gang had fled to be met by the chaotic scene abandoned by robbers who had shown no concern for the innocent victims of their crime.

The attacks then became more frequent. On 7 June, a post office worker was attacked with an iron bar and threatened with a revolver at Shawlands Shopping Centre and a bag with £21,800 in cash was stolen. The gang then returned to a hospital wages office, raiding the Southern General Hospital on 1 July when six staff were assaulted with firearms and a hammer.

This audacious gang were in action yet again early in the morning of 8 August at a post office in the Milton housing scheme. Once again, they had clearly planned their raid with precision. Four armed men waited in the cul-de-sac in front of the Westray Circus post office knowing there was to be a delivery of cash. Screaming threats at the post office worker, the four men armed with sawn-off shotguns stole £6,715 in cash.

These regular robberies began to attract copycat raids. Serious Crime Squad officers were now on regular patrol in the Greater Glasgow area in the hope of intercepting the raiders. Each squad car had three detectives and, because of the violence of the attacks, we were all armed. The early morning raid at Westray Circus was only a few miles from the previous Ruchill Hospital robbery – these guys were brazen and determined to keep going.

We were not far from catching them after the 8 August post office raid. That morning Jimmy Paul, Willie Kelly and I were patrolling the north of the city when the Westray Circus robbery was first reported over the radio. Jimmy was driving, as he trusted neither Willie nor me to get him to the scene safely. When we arrived at the Westray Circus, the post office worker was still in a state of shock and passers-by were keen to help and give statements. However, we knew our first duty was to try to track down the robbers and we set off in pursuit. From the previous raids, we anticipated that they always changed cars very near to the scene of the crime. We found their first getaway car very quickly, less than a quarter of a mile away. It was down a dead-end road which led to a path, where they would have left their second car parked on a main road. The abandoned car's engine was warm. We had been just a few minutes from catching them.

When we returned to the post office it looked like a scene from *The Bill*. Uniform police officers were securing the scene, detectives were taking statements from the witnesses and the members of the 'Saturday Sammie Club' had gathered to offer their wisdom to anyone who would listen to their ramblings.

We returned to our home station at Temple to review what we had ascertained and what needed to be done. The boss of the squad, John Blincow, was not happy. Hit by now weekly raids, the squad was not getting results. Blincow wanted action. Norrie Walker, his right-hand man, was known for his impatience. He was the practical man who made the boss's big ideas happen – but for once they were both struggling to make any impact against this gang. We lacked hard evidence and good intelligence.

14
False Leads and a
Little Bit of Luck

At the Serious Crime Squad office we started to piece together what we had gathered from the various robberies – and it wasn't much. What it did tell us, though, was that we had a team of robbers who mixed and matched their members and used a variety of weapons to confuse the police. It was clear, from the lack of evidence left at the scenes, that the group had planned their raids meticulously, particularly their getaways. One of them must have surveyed their targets beforehand – later I was to discover the planner's identity and would be told in great detail how things were decided.

A review of the likely suspects revealed the usual names but there was something different about this group. There appeared to be a large number of them, as there were different descriptions at various jobs. However, they always escaped in the same manner. Using a stolen car, they drove only a short distance from the raid. Then there was a brisk walk or run through some sort of physical barrier, such as a bridge over a river or a motorway. After that they would escape in a second, usually hidden, car. Their method of escape proved to be one of the few common denominators in the series of crimes; another was a connection to the Milton area of the city, near where many of the crimes were committed.

During the year, we received snippets of information

about a group of criminals who were living well. Although in the 1970s the sums stolen in total were quite substantial, the group was obviously up to some other scams as well.

The names Norval, O'Hara, Henry and Polding were given repeatedly as people we should be interested in. Norval was a blast from the past. He was thought to have largely disappeared from the criminal scene and many rated him as past it. He was known to rent out many of the cheap flats in the north side of the city and, during the 1950s, had had links with the Glasgow criminal underworld. It was difficult to work out Norval's involvement in the raids, given that he was 49 years old and that he was said to walk with a limp.

We were also receiving tip-offs suggesting future targets and dates for robberies, which we followed through in the hope of catching the robbers in full flow. In one case, we were told the gang planned to attack a wages office at a bus garage in Helen Street during the early hours. Large sums of cash were stored every Friday morning to pay the staff at around 8am. Information indicated that the gang, armed with shotguns, planned an attack at 7am.

The garage was on an open site, larger than two football fields, on the east side of Helen Street in Govan. As there was a police vehicle garage on the other side of the street, we had an easy, secure place to sit and wait. The boss, Blincow, was determined that we would be there to welcome the robbers on this occasion. His deputy, Norrie Walker, even insisted that, despite his seniority, he was going to come on the strike.

We had arranged to meet up at the Helen Street police garage at 4am on the morning of the expected robbery, having left our unmarked police cars there the night before. Around a dozen of us were to be there and such days were never easy to prepare for. I didn't sleep well on those nights as I would lie awake going over our plans and trying to work out each possible outcome. Like all my colleagues, I spent the night watching the clock so that I wouldn't sleep in.

When 3am finally arrived, I got up and dressed for the day's action. When there was the possibility of serious trouble, I always woke my wife to say goodbye – you never knew what was going to happen.

Once at the garage a dozen sleepy policemen needed a plan to distract us and Norrie Walker was just the man for that. First we were all issued with firearms. The bag of .38 revolvers and their leather shoulder holsters were spread on a worktop in the garage canteen to allow each officer to choose his weapon and select ammunition. Having chosen a weapon, each officer then had to note the serial number in his notebook and on a control sheet. The number of rounds issued to each officer was also recorded. We were usually given five or six rounds depending on the size of the chamber in the pistol. The long-nosed .38 took six rounds to fill the revolving chamber whilst the snub-nosed took five. I remember on this occasion being given double the usual allocation because of the growing violence of the gang's recent attacks. Norrie always wanted the long-barrelled .38 weapon – he had a particular preference for it as he believed it gave him a better chance of hitting his target.

I preferred the smaller .38 revolver. It wasn't as heavy to carry and I felt that it was likely that I would be close to my target before I would need to shoot. I thought the smaller gun offered me better protection, as well as a better chance of hitting the target.

As the firearms were being issued and the paperwork completed, I recalled a detective sergeant one night years earlier telling me about the Springburn shooting of James Griffiths by a police officer, Malcolm Findlayson, whom I met a year after the shooting.

Griffiths was an infamous criminal who went on a shooting spree across Glasgow in 1969 in an effort to evade capture. He was finally shot dead by a police officer. This detective sergeant had been a member of the Flying Squad at the time and he told me how the city was gripped by panic that afternoon as Griffiths went around the north of Glasgow shooting people as he tried to escape from the police.

In his final desperate bid to elude arrest Griffiths had taken refuge in an empty top-floor flat in Kay Street, Springburn, overlooking a children's playground. As the police moved in to try and arrest Griffiths, he started taking pot shots at people in the area and was even firing into the playground. The detective sergeant had been scrambled from his office in St Andrew's Square, just off the Saltmarket, grabbing all his equipment, including a firearm in its leather case, before rushing to the scene.

At Kay Street, he climbed on to a nearby rooftop which gave him the perfect position overlooking Griffiths, who was still firing recklessly at police and passers-by. Having got himself in prime position, the officer dropped below the apex of the roof to prepare his gun ready to shoot Griffiths. Safe in the knowledge he was out of sight, the intrepid detective sergeant reached inside his leather case and retrieved his binoculars! In his excitement to leave his office he had confused his leather cases and, although he had the best view of Griffiths of any police officer at scene, there was nothing he could do about him.

The detective sergeant's sorry tale taught me how important it was on such occasions to keep a cool head and always check my equipment. It was these simple things that could save people's lives.

Norrie's plan was simple: 'The fastest runners join me in the first car with the rest of you in the two cars behind. We will drive at high speed on to the garage site and arrest the robbers.' Norrie was fifty-seven and couldn't be described as fit; but woe betide anyone who would try and leave him behind. I was keen to be in the lead car if I was going to have any impact on the raid. The plan was clear and straightforward but we had all reckoned without a new colleague who felt the need for chapter and verse on the precise deployment. The officer made the fatal mistake of asking one question too many, trying Norrie's patience. He wanted to know how we would recognise the robbers and what we should do once we had arrested them. The frustrated Norrie told the youngster: 'This isn't a mannequin parade, son. When you see them, you'll recognise them. Just fucking arrest them and let's get home!'

The rest of the morning was to pass without comment and even less action. The robbers failed to keep their appointment and we were all left tired and disappointed. Stake-outs like this were to go on for some weeks without any success.

A number of the squad officers had informants who were supplying details about the robberies, but the information was fragmented and short of what we needed to take action. It was time therefore to try to get an overview of all the evidence. I was chosen to pull together the reports and analyse everything we had. We had partial identities of robbers, which was only enough to justify a prosecution if each of the witnesses linked their identifications to the same person. We also had some forensic evidence – fingerprints, paint, hairs and fibres linked to different scenes. What we needed, though, was a suspect to link to these samples. Finally, and crucially, we had a statement identifying a car linked with Walter Norval that had been seen near to the Ruchill Hospital shortly after the robbery.

Individually each piece of evidence was worthless but together they started to stack up to something that would eventually make a case. What we needed was a killer witness, someone who could piece it all together. By this time I had amassed a huge amount of paperwork but little of knockout value.

We knew that a group from the city was involved and that Norval seemed to play some part in the crimes. I knew that Norval had a number of in-laws with a criminal background, particularly Bill Gunn and Danny Fish. John McDuff, another repeat offender, was also connected to the family as were a number of Govan-based criminals including Joe Polding and Fred O'Hara.

By the time I had finished pulling together the various strands of the enquiry, we had what looked more like a devil's cauldron than a criminal conspiracy. What I really needed, though, was evidence and witnesses. I have learned over the years that the harder you work the luckier you get. The crew at the Serious Crime Squad worked hard; not only were we able to prove the links between each of the criminals involved but detective officers were beginning to extend the links to a man named Philip Henry, who was already wanted for his part in a jeweller's shop break-in in Glasgow.

It was now time to sit tight and be patient. Our break was to come within months and in the most unlikely of ways. Fortunately for us, the gang had begun to believe their own publicity and thought themselves above the law. Three of them went to raid a post office in Buckie, just north of Aberdeen. They had intended to steal car tax discs, TV licences and stamps to give them some extra spending money – any cash they found would just be a bonus.

As usual when Glasgow neds take a day trip out in the country, they left themselves wide open to arrest and Grampian police duly obliged. I was dragged from bed on 27 August to be told that Phil Henry, Fred O'Hara and Alan Barbour were in Grampian's custody in Buckie. Any one of these men would have been a great capture but catching all three was an amazing bonus. Indeed Barbour, a long-term criminal, was a new name to add to our list of suspects.

Jimmy Paul, Willie Kelly and I were sent up to Buckie to interview our new friends. We couldn't get up the road quick enough. I don't know how long it took but I'm sure the Stig from *Top Gear* would have struggled to have done it much faster. We arrived to find three belligerent prisoners who became even more unhappy when they saw who had turned up to interview them.

15

A Walk on the Wild Side

As the senior detective, Jimmy Paul was the first to question our three prisoners. He spooked them so much that neither O'Hara nor Henry would speak while he was in the room. Barbour, a career criminal, played the interview for everything he could get out of it. He was cagey throughout, trying to work out what we had in terms of evidence against him and others whilst trying not to give anything away. He would say anything to get himself out of trouble.

Once Jimmy left the room, Willie and I were able to work on the prisoners. Our journey north had given us time to discuss tactics. By the time we had the three settled into Grampian HQ in Aberdeen, we had a clear idea of what we wanted to do and how we were going to achieve it. We also had three prisoners all willing to talk but for very different reasons.

O'Hara had an extensive criminal background and had previously been a moneylender in Govan – not a career for the faint-hearted. He had several previous convictions but had also been acquitted of murdering a man in the middle of a public house in Govan. Given his fearsome reputation, he was not a man to be messed with. O'Hara had realised the game was up and that all hell was about to break loose. He also quickly realised that we three Glasgow detectives knew our 'specialised subject' – Glasgow robberies. Trying to avoid the coming onslaught, he quickly admitted to being involved in the robbery at the Westray post office and offered to help us to retrieve the firearms, which he said were hidden in a golf bag. He was trying to limit his involvement in the robberies to just one incident.

Alan Barbour tried a similar tack and admitted various crimes, in an attempt to limit his responsibility.

Meeting Philip Henry for the first time was an entirely different experience. An intelligent, tall, slim man, Henry was very nervous and anxious. He had spent the past year on the run from an outstanding warrant and constantly fidgeted with his small Van Gogh-style beard. Henry's eyes darted continually around the room searching into the eyes of his interrogators to try to make some connection. Within minutes, he had decided that he would not talk to the senior detective Jimmy Paul but once Jimmy had left the room he answered each of my questions. He appeared to be trying to judge whether he could trust Willie and me.

As the hours passed, Philip Henry relaxed as he realised that, though we knew he was a player, he was not the main target of our operation. As we talked, he declared his surprise at how much information we had about the robbers and their methods of working. At one point in our discussion he pulled on his beard deliberately and said he had decided to assist us. Phil had had enough of life on the run. I also suspect that, whilst other gang members had been enjoying the good life, Phil felt aggrieved because he had been forced to go into hiding because of his outstanding warrant.

Phil had also done a great deal of the preparatory work required to identify targets and the best method of carrying out specific robberies. He obviously felt he had received no recognition for his efforts from the rest of the gang. Finally and fatefully, some of the gang members had ridiculed his partner and this had got to him. He reckoned it was payback time.

Willie and I could not believe our luck. Not only did we have three members of the robbery team but one of them had decided to turn Queen's Evidence – willing to make a statement against his co-accused.

After a couple of hours (talking into the wee sma' hours), I decided enough was enough and it would be best to see Phil when we had all returned to Glasgow. Jimmy, Willie and I hightailed it back to Glasgow to feed the various enquiry teams with all the leads Phil had given us.

Back at our Glasgow office in Temple things were frenetic and the bosses were ecstatic. We were given whatever resources we needed. Half a dozen two-man teams followed up the snippets we had gleaned from the three prisoners. The work rate was phenomenal as each member of the squad was keen to play their full part in securing the evidence we needed.

By the time Phil had been brought down to Glasgow, Willie Kelly and I had been granted access to question him again. We were determined to make the best of it and thankfully Phil continued to see things in a similar way. When we met him in Glasgow, Phil wanted to take Willie and me out on to the Old Kilpatrick Hills where we could recover Walter Norval's gun and also some of the money stolen during the robberies.

So it was at 10 o'clock on the morning of Sunday, 28 August 1977 that Willie Kelly, Phil Henry and I began the climb up the Old Kilpatrick Hills in search of the money and guns. There was not another soul about.

Once we saw the climb ahead of us, Willie and I realised we had not come properly dressed but we didn't want to cause a delay in case Phil changed his mind and retracted his evidence. While the Glasgow detectives had their suits and 'dancing shoes' on, Phil was dressed in the tracksuit and trainers he had been wearing when he was arrested.

Phil Henry obviously enjoyed the sight of two police

officers slipping and sliding as we struggled to make our way up the hillside. The climb took the best part of two hours and the three of us spent the time discussing life, politics and the future.

Phil's whole life now depended on the outcome of the pending court case. He was well aware of the consequences of his decision to give evidence against his fellow criminals. He had been well respected amongst the Govan criminal fraternity and was known as a go-ahead thief willing to take risks. Phil knew that, in deciding to speak out against his criminal friends, his old lifestyle was at an end and he would remain a target until the day he died – but he had made his mind up. He was willing to plead guilty to his crimes but was clear that he was never going to take the blame for other criminals' activities or their crimes.

Willie and I also had a lot riding on this case. Our credibility as detectives would be judged on the outcome and we knew it was essential that we gathered the evidence and presented it in the correct fashion. We also knew that, behind the scenes, there were huge pressures being brought to bear to subvert our investigation. Witnesses were living in fear and, as quickly as we could gather evidence, alibis were being constructed.

Years later, in a letter from prison after his conviction, Phil told me that he had considered escaping during our day out on the hillside. Given our unsuitable footwear and clothes, he had realised that he could have easily escaped. He knew the hills well and was as fit as a fiddle. Whilst on the run, he had spent the best part of a year training every day and climbing these hills. However, because he liked the two of us, he decided to stay with us and complete the trip. I would not have been confident that Willie and I could have coped had Phil tried to do a runner. I also shudder at the thought of what would have happened to us had we returned to HQ without our prisoner.

Phil led us to near the top of the Old Kilpatrick Hills. Here he pointed to a path next to a tree where he had buried a bag with cash and a shotgun, which had been given to him by Norval. He had hidden the bag under the path because he reckoned that the farmers and gamekeepers would have spotted newly turned soil in an unspoilt part of the hills. In his view, there was less likelihood of anyone finding the bag under a path that was walked regularly.

Without Phil's help we would never have been able to find the spot and soon the three of us had dug up the hidden £3,500 in cash and a sawn-off shotgun. Phil formally identified them as being given to him by Walter Norval. Willie and I were tired but overjoyed that, after months of hard work, we both knew we were well on our way to halting this gang that had plagued Glasgow for so long.

As we headed back down the hillside with our evidence, Willie and I felt pleased with our Sunday morning hike. We were now able to take in the view and enjoy the countryside as we headed back down the steep inclines. However, it was obvious from Phil's face that he knew that it was going to be a long time before he could enjoy the freedom of his beloved hills again.

Phil still had one surprise at the end of that day, though. He wanted to make a voluntary statement detailing everything he knew about the gang's activities. He had decided it was time to clean his slate and he didn't want to leave anything hanging over him after the case was completed. Procedure dictated that neither Willie nor I could be involved in taking this statement. This was handed over to other officers and we were left wondering what Phil would say next.

We needn't have worried. During the following few days, Norval's empire and gang crumbled under the weight of evidence collected after Phil's voluntary statement. Later that week, Walter Norval, not long returned from an overseas holiday, and eight of his associates were arrested over the robberies. John 'Plum' McDuff and Joe Polding, Walter's key associates, were arrested in early morning swoops by the Serious Crime Squad. Fred O'Hara and Alan Barbour were already in custody, having been lifted in Grampian along with Phil Henry. A number of other men, including members of Norval's extended family, were also arrested.

At this stage, my contact with Phil was cut off. Given the imminent prosecution, it would have been improper for me to have contact with him while he was remanded in Barlinnie Prison awaiting trial.

As the time of the court case neared, the city was awash with rumours and speculation. There was also huge media interest in the case with newspapers all competing for the best coverage. The Glasgow public were at last satisfied that the police had taken action to halt the gang who had been terrorising the city.

16
Why the Gang was Really
Called the XYY Mob

As the trial date approached I was selected to be the liaison officer with the Crown. It was my job to ensure that all productions and statements were delivered to the Crown on time. Given my knowledge of the whole case against the men, I was the ideal candidate for the job. It was one of the first occasions such a role had been created. Given the scale of the charges and the amount of evidence it was difficult to imagine how a prosecutor would have been able to handle the case without such support.

Because of this complexity, it was also decided that a single jury would be incapable of taking in all the evidence to be presented at a trial. The Crown Office therefore decided that the case would require at least four separate trials. The trials were to follow one after another and the four trials would take at least five weeks to complete.

To add to the complications, some of the accused involved in the early trials also faced charges relating to the later cases. Because of the massive media interest, there was a real danger that a jury would be aware of decisions or evidence given in the earlier trials. So the Crown decided to tag all of the accused with a particular letter to ensure they could receive a fair trial individually, whether they had been convicted or cleared at one of the preceding trials. This is the real reason they became known as the XYY mob and the media thereafter used the XYY headline to reflect that some of the un-named accused would appear more than once on indictments. In the years since the trials there have been many other spurious explanations about how the gang got their name, so it's worth clearing this up.

During this time, Phil Henry had placed himself 'on protection' at Barlinnie Prison. Protection was usually provided to sexual offenders but later Phil told me about the intimidation he faced during the run-up to the trials. As well as keeping himself locked up in his own cell all day, Phil refused to eat his prison meals as he expected them to be contaminated or spat upon. The fitness fanatic, who had the previous year run in the Old Kilpatrick Hills, had to survive on a diet of chocolate bars for almost a year in Barlinnie.

There were also scuffles outside his cell and notes passed under his door. These notes threatened him, his family and his girlfriend if he gave evidence for the prosecution. Others made him various offers, if he did the 'right thing'.

As the trials approached there was much speculation across the city that Phil Henry would not make it to court. No one, other than Phil himself, knew exactly what he was going to do or say. The underworld let it be known that Phil was actually going to go into the box to scupper the prosecution case in front of the jury.

There were also many threats made against other witnesses. In the run-up to the trials, I and other police officers spent a great deal of time visiting people who were being intimidated and were worried about what would happen after they had given evidence.

There was yet more high drama on the eve of the trials. I was woken early on the Monday morning by a phone call from my boss, John Blincow. 'They've attacked the High Court. They've tried to burn it down,' he said and told me to get down there right away. When I put the phone down I hadn't taken in what he really said.

I arrived in the early hours of the morning to find the fire service still hosing down and clearing up. Most of the Serious Crime Squad was there, as were senior detectives from Central division, which was responsible for policing the area around the court. It was clear from the start that a fire had been started deliberately. It was no accident but an attempt to destroy evidence stored in the court building. Later, the forensic examination proved that an accelerant had been used in the fire. Although badly damaged, the North Court could be saved. Fortunately for us all our productions from the trials were safe. The authorities were increasingly determined to show that the course of justice could not be diverted by the fire. Our cases against those known now as the XYY mob were to go ahead as planned in the South Court.

The suspicions about who might be to blame for the court fire ratcheted up the pressure even further for those involved in the cases. By the time Phil Henry stepped into the witness box to give evidence, you could have heard a pin drop in the concourse of the court building.

Phil was brought directly into the court away from the other prisoners and marched between two police officers through the building. Although I did not see him arrive, by all accounts he was highly irritable and nervous. This was understandable. The High Court had not been a friendly place for him in the past. Now he was returning to face the fellow members of his gang – this time to give evidence against them.

As if that was not enough, the public gallery was full of friends and relatives of the accused who were waiting anxiously to watch Phil give his evidence. They were to be disappointed – the trial judge took the extraordinary step at that time of clearing the public galleries.

As he started to give his evidence, Phil began to tug nervously on his goatee beard. He admitted all of the charges he was facing and then started to outline his evidence against his former gang members. Even that morning the gossip in the prison van bringing the XYY mob down to court was that Phil Henry was 'going to stick it to' the detectives from the Squad and blow apart the whole prosecution case. Even after he started giving evidence, the corridors of the court were full of rumours that he was not going to play his part.

Although hesitant at first, Phil soon showed his mettle. As soon as he felt the defence advocates were making a fool of him, Phil retaliated. He revealed everything he knew about the accused and the most damaging was about Norval. By the time a confident, and even triumphant, Phil Henry had finished giving his evidence and left the court building, he could have taught the top lawyers about the best way to deliver devastating evidence.

When I saw Phil a few days later he was calm and collected. He told me that he had not been looking forward to his day in court. However, he felt that, if he was to have any future, he needed to put the trial behind him. He was glad to have cleared the air.

The effect of his evidence on the XYY mob was clear to see. These loud, confident jokers became quiet and sullen. Along with everyone involved in the case, they knew that our evidence, the various witnesses' identifications and the small pieces of forensic evidence was not in itself sufficient to get convictions. However, when this was put alongside Phil's damaging testimony, there was clearly enough.

Waiting for the jury's decision is never an easy time. The defence had presented a catalogue of allegations against the police ranging from corruption to incompetence and a series of alibis designed to confuse the jury.

Finally, the jury foreman returned with guilty verdicts against Norval, McDuff, Polding, O'Hara, Barbour and

McDowall. Lord Cowie sentenced the mob to a total of seventy-four years in jail with Plum McDuff receiving a twenty-one year term. Phil Henry received four years and I have no doubt he would have received a substantially longer sentence had he not given evidence in the trial.

Throughout his time in prison as a convicted prisoner, I corresponded regularly with Phil. I knew that he faced a very difficult time in the prison system. Our final letters were exchanged when he was released and he had settled in a new life elsewhere. I haven't heard from him since.

17
Plum McDuff
Goes on the Run

There were a few loose ends to be dealt with in the aftermath of the XYY mob trials in Glasgow but a few months later I had thought that would be the last we'd hear from this gang. Plum McDuff had other ideas.

Two years after his conviction, the ever-ingenious McDuff escaped from Perth Prison. Along with another Category A prisoner (prisoners identified as requiring specific security because of the threat they present either of escaping or violence), one night he scrambled over a prison wall.

I knew the details of the escape from the usual police circulars and had asked around their usual hang-outs to try to find out if the pair had turned up in Glasgow. There was no word of them. The received wisdom was that McDuff and William Manson, another well-known Glasgow criminal, would be out of Scotland by now. Two months had passed without a sighting and, as a result, I also began to think they had escaped the country.

I was at home on 30 December, helping with the family New Year arrangements for a change, when I received an unusual phone call from the duty officer in the police headquarters control room. A man had called and asked me to ring a public phone box if I wanted to catch John

McDuff. The inspector didn't know what it was all about and wondered if I wanted to make the call! When I rang the number I was told that McDuff and Manson had arrived in Glasgow that very day. They had been in hiding near Perth since their escape. I was given two addresses on the north side of the city, both known to me, where I was told I should look for them. It was a very strange call but not one I was going to ignore.

I rang Davie Frew, who had taken over as boss of the Serious Crime Squad, and told him what I knew. Returning to duty, we rounded up our Squad colleagues before heading off to the first address. We missed the pair by minutes. However, we were told that both escaped prisoners were carrying briefcases containing loaded shotguns. Clearly, they were determined not to have to return to prison.

The second address was in Milton, a housing estate in the north of Glasgow. I knew it well. The terraced house was the home of Walter Norval's daughter, Rita, a place where McDuff would have expected to receive a warm welcome.

We had an extremely threatening situation. A dangerous, armed escaped prisoner was hiding out in a family home, with children sleeping in the adjoining rooms. Davie Frew, I have to say, was just the man for such a tricky job. He had the experience and the knowledge required to plan our next moves and follow them through.

Davie knew I had been in the house and that I knew the family. He asked me if I could get into the house and into the bedroom in which McDuff was likely to be sleeping. I was confident I could. So with Davie Frew right behind me, it was decided that I would lead the raid through the front door and up the stairs. At the same time a second team would break in the back and cover the ground floor.

The waiting is always the worst part. As we sat in the car in a nearby street waiting for a couple of hours, the nerves were jangling. Officers from the Support Unit were pouring into the area; the dog branch was nearby standing ready should the prisoners try to escape yet again.

When the time came, we drove round to the front of the house and, as we went as quietly as possible to our positions, all I could hear was the sound of the police dogs barking in the distance. Standing ready at the front door with Davie Frew at my side, I had a moment of doubt – surely our escapees would have been awoken by the dogs?

One of the guys kicked in the front door with a single deliberate blow; I was surprised how easily it gave way. With my pistol in my right hand, I moved to the left of the hall in the pitch darkness looking for the tread of the first step. I knew the master bedroom was at the front of the house. As I raced up the stairs, I could feel Davie's hand in the middle of my back supporting me. I could see nothing in the darkness but as I ran I kept looking for the flash of a shotgun. Having thought the dogs would have woken McDuff, I expected to be greeted by him at the top of the stairhead.

Seconds later, I was at the top of the landing. I turned right and kicked in the bedroom door as hard as I could. I rushed into the room. In the dim light I could see a man darting to the side of the bed and wrestling with something black. I hit McDuff as hard as I could on the side of his face with my revolver and Davie jumped on top of him, dragging him away from what turned out to be the briefcase containing the loaded shotgun. It was all over in seconds. Suddenly it went quiet; we had McDuff but there was no sign of Manson.

Within minutes the house was full of police officers and the children were all screaming. McDuff and Rita Norval were both arrested. McDuff was taken away to Maryhill police office where I charged him in relation to his escape, the possession of the firearm and other related offences. He was shocked at the suddenness of his arrest after his months at liberty.

As we took the lift to the cell passageway, I asked the turnkey if he could give me a moment with McDuff on my own. I had expected that the officer would stand outside the cell in the passageway but instead he led us to the cell and, after I had entered, he slammed the door behind us and left the two of us alone.

McDuff was now an injured, worn-out and lonely soul. Although we had been on opposite sides for many years, when I sat with him in his cell that night we were able to have a sensible conversation. I truly felt sorry for him.

Here was a man who had had few opportunities to do anything other than become a criminal. Yet here, in his darkest hour, his main concern was whether he could maintain his credibility with the other Category A prisoners.

When I asked him about Manson's whereabouts, he explained that he had a lifetime of prison time to serve and I realised there was little point in trying to press him further. Here we were on New Year's Eve, a policeman and criminal sharing a cell. He was facing yet another sentence to add to his twenty-one-year term. I wished him a Happy New Year and left him with his thoughts.

Later that day, I learned we had missed Manson by just a few hours. McDuff and Manson had spent the evening together but Manson had left to bunk down at another house in Milton. Of course, as soon as he had been alerted to our early morning raid he had done a runner.

Months later, I was on duty night shift when a dog branch officer, near to the Baillieston area of the city, came across a man hiding near a park. After a monumental struggle between the two men, the officer managed to overcome the man and arrest him. I was radioed to get down to the Royal Infirmary to meet this man, who refused to speak.

There was Manson lying tight-lipped in a bed. He was in

such a fit of pique at being caught that he refused to speak or even acknowledge his identification. Soon, Manson was back in prison.

Many years later, in 2007, I saw Walter Norval again in Glasgow. He was just walking through the crowded city centre streets and passed within inches of me. I couldn't believe how well he looked after all these years. After all the harm and stress he had caused to so many innocent victims of his crimes, he was now out having served his sentence and paid his dues. As with Phil Henry, I have heard no more of his activities and trust that his life of crime is now behind him. Though I know that, to this day, there is still no love lost between Walter and Phil.

18

Shotguns, Stake-outs and the UVF

The last few days of 1977 were an exciting time for me as I had just taken up a new promoted post at the Central CID based in Stewart Street. However, Christmas Eve turned out to be far more exciting than I would have liked.

I was still in my new office at 10pm on Christmas Eve when I received an anonymous phone call. A very well-spoken lady told me she had seen two men, one armed with a gun, around Nevis Road in Bearsden. Although she was very polite, the woman refused to give her name or explain further but she thought that the two men were about to commit a robbery. I gave her my personal assurance that I would do everything in my power to prevent the robbery and I would be heading out to Nevis Road myself.

I knew that, late on Christmas Eve, it was going to be very difficult for us to respond appropriately. Most of the police on duty were committed. It was also questionable as a force whether we should respond at all to something on the basis of anonymous information. I had been the only person to have spoken to the woman – but there was something about her that had impressed me.

The only chance to put together a group of officers at such an ungodly hour was to call on my former colleagues at the Serious Crime Squad based in nearby Temple police station. When I called, it was not the regular shift that had worked with me. Willie Christie, the duty detective sergeant, promised to send his crew, despite some of them being due to head off for their well-deserved Christmas break with their families.

As ever, they all volunteered to stay on and, by the time I drove out to Bearsden, Willie and his team were there in unmarked cars having collected their firearms. The area proved to be challenging and it was difficult to make out the houses in the dark in the built-up streets around Nevis Road.

There were seven us and Willie Christie, Ronnie Edgar and I were in an unmarked Mini. We parked it next to some open ground opposite Nevis Road and we had already seen two men pass by carrying what looked like a stick. They had passed us on the road and had gone into the back garden of one of the houses.

I had rarely worked with this group from the Squad but they showed the same commitment and passion to getting on with the job that I had enjoyed with other colleagues.

On this dark December night we could sit in our car virtually unseen. With the engine switched off, the condensation was soon running down the windows, giving us even better cover. We were going to be extremely unlucky to be spotted. The other two cars were further out of the area so they could report any other comings and goings and we kept in contact through our scrambled radios.

Stake-outs can be very tedious. Officers who want to be in the thick of the action and are used to being on the go, suddenly find themselves grounded waiting for something to happen. Stake-outs can go on for minutes, hours, days and sometimes much longer.

My longest was from Friday afternoon until Monday morning. It was back in my Easterhouse days. Jimmy Lindsay and I sat in a police car in Lochdochart Road as we waited over a September weekend for a wanted criminal to turn up. We knew he had been driving a stolen car with false plates. Having found the car hidden away, neither of us was prepared to give up until he showed up to collect it. By the Sunday, the car was beginning to smell dreadful. We kept ourselves going on an unhealthy diet from the local chip vans. On Monday lunchtime we arrested our man, who was shocked to be apprehended by Glasgow's two smelliest detectives. We were just delighted to get our man, although we did suffer a terrible ribbing once we got back to the office.

My Bearsden stake-out was going to be much shorter, whatever happened, as I had promised my colleagues that, if there was no action by midnight, we would all head home. At the back of my mind I was also slightly worried I had been set up and would end up having to apologise for holding them back from their families on Christmas Eve. When I admitted my reservations to Willie, he was his normal upbeat self and would have none of it.

As usual, nothing worked to script. The two men with the stick reappeared suddenly in the open ground next to our car. We became aware of them standing and talking right next to our car. As they did, I bent forward to the driver's side of the car and lay with my face down in Willie's lap, so they couldn't see me. As I sat face down, we all heard the distinctive sound of a pump-action shotgun being loaded. Willie whispered to me that, should he die, he didn't want his family to worry about my face being buried in his crotch at the time of his death.

Thankfully, the men soon started heading off towards Nevis Road. As Willie and I sat up, we could see the men, their heads now covered by balaclavas, walking towards a nearby house. Willie, Ronnie and I, armed with our police-issue batons, jumped out the car but, as soon as we did, the two men saw us.

As we moved towards them, the two stood their ground.

One of them, who we later identified as George Seawright, a twenty-year-old from nearby Drumchapel, pointed his shotgun at all three of us. His colleague, later revealed to be David Briggs, shouted: 'Shoot the Provo bastards.'

Fortunately, Seawright hesitated. We didn't. We just rushed straight at him. After a violent and noisy struggle, Seawright dropped the shotgun. It fell on to the road under a parked car. As the three of us instinctively turned to watch the gun fall, the two would-be robbers took off.

The locals, who only a few minutes before had been preparing for Christmas, were standing at their windows watching the action. Seawright and Briggs split up, heading in different directions. I stayed with Briggs and after about ten metres managed to drag him to the ground. With the help of my colleagues from the other cars which had just arrived, I arrested him. Ronnie Edgar caught up with Seawright at the back door of a nearby house and, after a short exchange of blows, he was also arrested.

As we led the men away to the local police office, they seemed relieved that they had been arrested by the police and were not being dealt with by the Provisional IRA. The men had had a few drinks, to give them Dutch courage, before setting out on their job and had mistakenly thought that we were members of another paramilitary group there to ambush them.

In his excitement, Seawright was particularly keen to tell us that he was a lieutenant in the Ulster Volunteer Force and, along with his partner Briggs, was out collecting funds for the cause. They didn't want to be thought of as mere common criminals. He admitted that he had been sent out to rob a businessman in Nevis Road and had anticipated stealing more than £5,000 in cash. We wished the two of them a Merry Christmas, spent locked up in a police cell, before heading off to see our families. Later it became clear that the two had been targeting a house belonging to a local coal merchant.

Some months later, we were all surprised to discover there was going to be a trial at the High Court in Glasgow. Their defence was that they had been waiting innocently at a nearby bus stop when Serious Crime Squad officers arrested them and a pump-action shotgun was planted on them. Ridiculous as this might seem, defences like this are presented every day in our courts, usually at huge cost to the taxpayer. After hearing the police evidence, the jury convicted both the men. Later it became apparent that Seawright had very strong connections, through his extended family, with people involved in Northern Ireland politics.

For me, 1977 had been a crucial year. It was the year I discovered the value of comradeship. I saw how police officers would stand together, no matter the pressures and stresses, and see things through. In some ways this period demonstrates the best of police work. There was no rationale in these officers delaying their Christmas break to join me in Bearsden. Equally, there was no reason why they should place themselves in danger for some unknown coal merchant from Bearsden. They were willing to do it because it was their duty. If they didn't turn out, who would?

Too often budgets overlook nights such as this one and the work done in the public interest. Frequently we rush to understand the cost of a service and not its true value.

19
A Clear-cut Case

My return to the Central division had been very much a homecoming for me. I knew many of the staff extremely well and I also knew the area like the back of my hand. The work was much the same as before, except we were all required to do more to tackle the higher level of reported crime. From the office in Stewart Street, a new building near the abandoned site of my first office in the old Northern divisional headquarters, I spent most of the time dealing with car thefts, shop break-ins and violent attacks.

A few weeks after the Bearsden robbery, I was back on the city streets. As the new detective sergeant I had a group of detective constables to work alongside. One was Bob Lauder, and he and I became a regular feature around the city as we competed to see who could put in the longest hours on the job. Bob was always first in the office each morning as he sought to select the pick of the overnight reports for us to investigate.

I preferred the afternoon and night shifts, as this was always the best time to catch criminals. Between us we had virtually every twenty-four-hour period covered with Bob in the office early and me working on late into the night. Once we had gathered the necessary information we would then operate as a team to arrest our suspects. Many years later, Bob was to become my deputy at the Scottish

Drug Enforcement Agency where we repeated our working partnership to great effect.

As well as Bob's daily fishing in the routine crime reports, we also had reports allocated to us by the CID clerk. It was one of these reports that led me one Monday morning to a Hope Street office, near to Central Station, an area which had been hit by a spate of office break-ins.

Typically, the thief hid in the premises and came out only after the staff had gone home or broke into the offices over a weekend when the staff would not be at work. Although the Stewart Street detectives were aware of the break-ins, we had no leads to help us identify the offenders.

Such crimes were usually committed by young people, who could then wander around the city centre at weekends or in the early evenings virtually unseen. In the days before closed-circuit television, it was very difficult to keep tabs on everyone loitering around the main railway station.

What was different about these break-ins, though, was the type of goods being stolen. Office equipment, telephone exchanges, photocopiers and similar valuable machines were being taken regularly – but where were they being sold? There must be a shop or somewhere else selling them, as they were not the type of goods that could be sold around the doors of a housing estate or by an advert in the snips page of the local paper.

The site of the latest break-in was a huge meandering Victorian building that covered an area the size of a football park. Inside were hundreds of single or double rooms rented out to individual businesses.

There was no way of checking who might have been in this vast warren of businesses at the time of the crime and the offices did not even have an alarm system. The doors forced to gain entry were along a corridor and out of view of the public.

On this occasion, phones, calculators and small sums of

WARD WINNER: My father, Jimmy Pearson, being presented with a rose bowl for being the best carter.

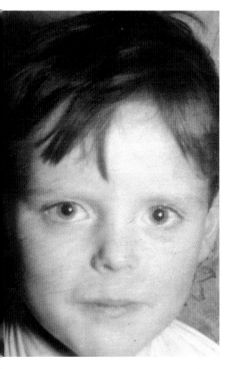

PARTICK BOY: Graeme Pearson, aged six, ken after a professional photographer came to our door in Fordyce Street.

MARCH 1970: Starting work as a police probationer.

FRANKIE VAUGHAN: He was involved in a high-profile campaign to bring peace to Easterhouse.

ROBERT MONE: In his trademark coat which he was wearing on the night of the Carstairs murders.

THOMAS McCULLOCH: Mone's partner in crime being led away under police escort.

THREE OF A KIND: Walter Norval, Plum McDuff and Joe Polding, the three leaders of the XYY mob.

ARTHUR THOMPSON AND HIS WIFE: Arthur traded stolen silver in a late night meeting in Glasgow's East End.

GARTNAVEL MURDERER: Triple killer John Harkins who killed his wife, son and brother-in-law.

HEADING FOR COURT: Willie Williamson and Graeme Pearson heading Glasgow High Court for the Triad trial.

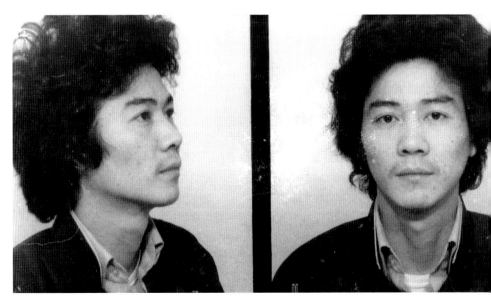

CHAN KING WING: He was jailed and then deported in Scotland's first Triad case.

MARK McMANUS: Taggart who more than amply repaid the little help I gave him.

NYPD: Detective Gerry McQueen who showed me the real side of New York.

ON CAPITOL HILL: Visiting the FBI headquarters, good friends to Scotland.

IN THE PICTURE: The launch of the CCTV system in Airdrie Police Station.

©Mirrorpix.com

DIPLOMACY IN EASTERHOUSE: A Prince and President visit the Glasgow scheme.

©Richard Newton Photography

CHOICES FOR LIFE: Teaching youngsters about drugs in a way they really understand.

©SNS Group

HEAD OF THE SCDEA: Speaking at a
European money laundering conference
held in Glasgow.

MO JOHNSTON: Who turned
out to be Airdrie's best Santa Claus
for a group of deserving youngsters.

©PAPhotos.com

©PAPhotos.com

HOLOGRAM TAM McANEA and JOHN McGREGOR: Who were printing
banknotes in a shop in Glasgow's West End.

CADIZ HARBOUR: The cargo of the MV *Squilla*, eight tonnes of cannabis resin with a street value of £24m, which was seized as part of Operation Folklore.

OPERATION FOLKORE: John 'Piddy' Gorman, who was jailed for 12 years and his associa▮ who were jailed in Scotland and Spain (clockwise) – William McDonald, Mushtaq Ahmed, Jar Lowrie, Sufian Mohammed Dris, Arno Podder, William Reid and Douglas Prince.

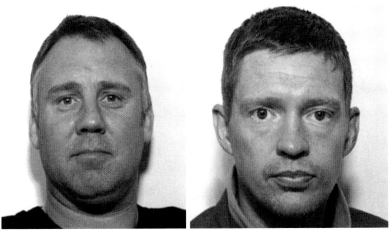

JAMIE STEVENSON and his key associate and stepson GERARD CARBIN: A prominen▮ criminal told police, "if you can get to Stevenson, you can get to any of us".

money had been taken. The offices had been locked on the Friday evening and the break-in had been discovered on Sunday morning.

A search of the premises revealed nothing for forensics and no fingerprints; on the face of it, the case looked like it had reached a dead end. My last chance was to speak to the man who discovered the break-in on the Sunday.

As was so often the case, my witness lived outside the city centre and proved difficult to track down. Later that day, when I did manage to speak to him, I discovered that he was a self-employed joiner, who had been working alone in the office complex that Sunday morning.

He had promised to do some work in one of the offices but had almost failed to make it because of his late night excesses on the Saturday. However, still under the weather but knowing that future jobs depended on keeping in with the factors, he had turned up around 10.30 on Sunday morning.

The joiner had found it slightly spooky working in the vast building all alone on a Sunday but there were other advantages. He could park his van without getting a ticket and make as much noise and mess as he needed to, without the office workers continually complaining.

No sooner had the joiner started to set up when he heard noises and then saw a man, wearing a dark coat with the hood raised, walk hurriedly past in the corridor. The joiner shouted after the man but he then heard him break into a run as he headed to the front entrance of the building.

The joiner gave chase as the man fled down Waterloo Street towards Hope Street before disappearing in Central Station. The witness then phoned the police but could only give them the broadest of descriptions. I was never going to be able to find a man wearing a duffel coat with a hood covering his face. The joiner was adamant he could be traced – what about getting a fingerprint from the spectacles he had dropped during the chase?

Having given up the chase, the joiner had retraced his steps to where he had seen the thief drop his glasses. Thinking they could be vital evidence, he had presented them to the police officer who had turned up at the scene. However, the report I received did not even mention the spectacles.

The officer, who had by this time finished his shift, was not too happy when I called him while he was off-duty to ask about the spectacles. He told me that I would find them in the found property box where he had put them, as he saw little chance of getting any fingerprints off them. Back at the station, I soon found the spectacles which were unusual and had thick, darkened lenses. The joiner confirmed they were the correct glasses but it was now too late to try to get any fingerprints from them.

Then I began to wonder – would a professional be able to recognize the glasses? I asked an optician who suggested I try a trade magazine. However, he did warn me that a picture of a pair of glasses would be of limited value. He also suggested I speak to Mr M. H. Wallace, the Chairman of the Western Ophthalmic Committee.

To my surprise, Mr Wallace was able to measure the lenses and the frame and all its dimensions. Taking the prescription details and the internal measurements of the spectacle frames together, Mr Wallace insisted, the accused could be identified with a great deal of confidence – similar to the unique footprint that we now associate with DNA. He was so persuasive that I circulated his detailed description of the spectacles to every optician across Scotland.

This became the butt of many office jokes and I received a terrible wind-up from my CID colleagues, who would ask me continually and mockingly whether my plea had had any response. Even I had almost given up hope when, months later, I was phoned one day by an optician in Gordon Street, just around the corner from the break-in.

That very day, the optician had ordered a replacement

pair of glasses, just like the set dropped at the scene. When I raced around to see him, I discovered his client was a businessman who worked in the building where the break-in had taken place. As it was a bank holiday weekend the businessman was not in his office, so I headed out to his home on the south side of Glasgow. There his wife told me he was out but, without telling her why I wanted to speak to him, I asked him to call me later.

When he rang, at first he was tentative but soon agreed to come and see me when I explained that I was investigating a break-in at the offices where he worked. When he arrived at Stewart Street, I knew immediately that he was my man, although I did not have sufficient evidence to proceed against him.

He was a very affable man in his thirties who ran a highly successful business but I was somewhat disconcerted to find he also sat on the Children's Panel. The reason that I was so confident it was him was that he was wearing glasses almost exactly the same as the pair recovered from the scene. He also had a very unusual way of responding to my questioning. He was extremely polite but failed to answer any of my direct questions. He seemed overly keen for me to know all about his respectability and his background but shied away from dealing with the circumstances surrounding the office break-in. In the end he was unable to explain the loss of his spectacles!

Eventually, the businessman acknowledged that the glasses were his and then went on to admit to the break-ins. He said that he carried them out as he wanted to experience the excitement he thought criminals felt during a crime. Dealing with the Children's Panel had exacerbated his problem and had pushed him over the line. He also told me where he had stashed all the stolen goods – in a lock-up near his home.

At court a few weeks later, the businessman pled guilty

to the break-ins and was jailed for almost a year. It wasn't the outcome I had anticipated. I thought he needed help rather than punishment. Later, I received a letter which had been written to the Chief Constable commending me for my successful investigation. The convicted businessman had written it from his cell.

Nearly thirty years later, just after I had announced my intention to retire from the police, I bumped into this same businessman in Buchanan Street, Glasgow. Despite the many years, he had hardly changed. I was pleased to learn that he hadn't been involved in crime since our meeting all those years ago and life had been very good to him.

20
Divine Intervention and the Height of Criminal Activity

It's not every day that a police officer tackles big-time crimes and for much of my service I dealt with bread and butter incidents on the streets of Glasgow. It is always important to remember that, though they might have been routine cases to a police officer, crime can have a life-changing impact on the victims.

Back in these old days a criminal investigation department was run essentially by a clerk. Usually he, and in those days it was always a he, was a senior constable who managed the incoming crime reports from uniform officers and incoming telephone calls. He then used a control sheet which was designed to share out the work fairly between the detectives. The clerk was someone you needed to keep on the right side of. If you upset the CID clerk then you could suddenly find yourself inundated with a series of difficult reports or the serial problematic complainers. Equally, if he knew you were working hard, he could ensure you received the straightforward crime reports, giving you the chance to clear your feet.

Most days the huge volume of reports meant there were too many to investigate them all properly. Thankfully many of the reports only required a little time to clear up. Most of the time they had been reported 'for insurance purposes only' or the complainer would not co-operate with the police. So, on many occasions I would find myself sent to interview a patient in the Glasgow Royal Infirmary, usually a man who had been stabbed, shot or battered the night before, to be told that I wasn't welcome nor would he give me any statement. I would always insist the patient sign my notebook. Thereafter I would investigate the matter no further although the report would still be logged in our system for future reference.

One Friday in October 1978, I was given my usual varied allocation of reports by old Neil, the CID clerk, including the theft of a large sum of cash from a pawnbroker's shop in Bath Street. The Glasgow Pawnbroking Company was on the first floor on the corner with Buchanan Street, and with my colleague Bob Lauder I made my way to investigate this mysterious theft. We arrived to find the shop owner had three trusted staff who had worked with him for a number of years. The four staff dispensed loans from behind a counter and stored the pawned goods out of the public's view.

The public had no access to the rear shop area as there was a sealed door and screens adjacent to the serving counter to prevent any robberies. The sole public access was the pawn booth, a small cupboard-sized room very like a confessional box. People pledging items would enter the room, close a door behind them and wait for the assistant to open a window to serve them. If a deal had been agreed the customer was given a pawn ticket explaining the terms but at no time did they have access to the pawnshop's back shop. There were even brass bars to prevent anyone crawling through the hatch.

The theft of a considerable sum of money in these circumstances narrowed down our field to four suspects. It surely had to be an inside job. After all, there were four people working in a space no bigger than a living room with a safe in the corner from which the cash had been stolen. Bob and I interviewed all the staff at length. They were all understandably nervous but all appeared believable and after a couple of hours we had got nowhere. Although we thought a forensic examination would be of little use, as all the staff had access to the safe, we wanted one just in case it threw up a clue. So with all questions answered by staff and a forensic exam organised, we were about to leave the pawnshop when it suddenly dawned on one of the staff that a window cleaner had been at the shop that morning and he might be a witness. He hadn't been inside the shop and they only knew his first name, Chris. So Bob and I set off on a long hunt to track down Chris the Glasgow window cleaner, who just might be able to solve this mysterious theft.

From the local businesses, Bob and I soon found out that Chris cleaned most of the windows in the area but, as he worked for himself and was normally paid cash, we had no calling cards to track him down. So we then went in search of any window cleaners we could find and finally in Buchanan Street, just off St Vincent Street, we tracked down a window cleaner who, although he didn't know Chris, suggested we head up to Curlers Bar in Byres Road where the window cleaners often met up.

Needless to say the window cleaners at the Curlers Bar were suspicious of us and thought we were working for the Department of Social Security and were looking for benefit dodgers. Finally, one young man said he knew a Chris from Castlemilk who worked in the city centre and he had a telephone number for him. After the necessary checks, Bob and I set off for Castlemilk but again we were out of luck. A committed Christian, Chris was out with his girlfriend doing charity work for his church. We could not trace him, so left a note asking him to ring us at Stewart Street police station. We both knew that, the longer we delayed, the less likelihood we had of recovering the cash, so it was with some reluctance that we put the case aside to catch up with our other reports.

On Saturday morning, in the middle of the guddle of clearing up the previous night's crime reports, Chris phoned. He insisted that he was unable to help and was very busy that morning so could he deal with the questions on the phone? There was something about his manner that made me want to question him face to face. He somewhat reluctantly agreed to take time to call by about midday and give me a statement but I started to become suspicious, as he still hadn't asked me what it was about or which business premises we were investigating.

At twelve o'clock a bright and pleasant well-built man in his early twenties with long, blond hair turned up. He was very nervous. As Bob and I questioned him about the previous morning, he still did not ask us what we were investigating. When I closed in on the pawnshop, he carefully explained he had cleaned all the outside windows and then moved on further down the street. He hadn't been inside the shop nor seen anything of note. When I asked about the theft, he said that as a Christian he would never have considered such a thing.

Then I boldly suggested to Chris that he had stolen the money and kept it for himself. Before he could respond I reminded him that, though he could pull the wool over my eyes, a greater power would be witnessing our conversation and know the truth. Chris had to live with his conscience and decide what was more important to him, the cash or his loyalty to God and his church. The room fell silent. Bob was struck dumb by my gallus approach; he thought I had finally lost the plot. How could an atheist like me dare to put such a suggestion to this window cleaner? But my bold appeal worked. After a few mumbling responses, Chris explained that the cash, with the exception of £40, was hidden in the car park opposite the police station. He had brought the money with him and with hindsight I think he must have been looking to admit his crime. Bob and I walked over to the nearby Cowcaddens car park and there, by the rear tyre of one of the cars, was a package containing the stolen cash.

There was great celebration at the pawnshop. The staff were all relieved that they were no longer suspects. It transpired that, while cleaning the windows, Chris had seen that the pawnshop safe had been left open by one of the staff who had been distracted by a telephone call. With all the other members of staff engaged in accepting pledges, Chris opened the window, climbed in and stole the cash. He was back out on the window ledge before anyone had noticed and then finished his usual day's work. At least Chris had made peace with his conscience, though with a conviction to his name as a result of the fine he received at the court.

Later that very same week, I was on late shift at the Central, which covers all crimes in the city. This meant dealing with the radio calls from uniformed officers who were in need of some CID support as well as requests from outside police forces.

My set of late shifts had been fairly busy but by overnight Thursday/Friday the wet weather had quietened the streets. It was a given in the police that rain was the best crime prevention measure around. Nevertheless there are always some criminals who will go out no matter the weather. Around 1.30 on Friday morning the alarm sounded at the premises of Hamilton Laidlaw, a well-known wholesale jeweller's store just off Argyle Street. The large store occupied five or six floors of an impressive nineteenth-century red sandstone building. Within minutes of the alarm going off, several officers were at the store awaiting the arrival of the keyholder. At first it just appeared a false alarm. Then one of the officers checked the front door and realised that the locks had been filled with glue to make them unusable.

I had arrived on the scene with a uniformed colleague who had been seconded to the department to learn the ropes and there were also another four uniformed officers there. As we started discussing what to do we could hear glass breaking from inside the building and stage whispers coming from high up on the roof. As usual, I was becoming impatient. I knew we had thieves but I couldn't get to them and it looked as if they were going to escape over the rooftops.

I could also hear another persistent and annoying engine noise nearby and, when I went to investigate, I saw that further down Argyle Street there was a Strathclyde fire engine with a large turntable ladder on the back. The crew were packing up after answering a false fire alarm at a department store. This seemed the answer to our problem – the turntable ladder would give access to the roof and the opportunity to arrest the crooks. The lead firefighter agreed to move the engine and, within a few minutes, the ladder was being extended on to the roof of the jeweller's. At that moment I felt full of admiration for the fire service and stood back to await the crew's ascent which, I thought, would allow us to enter the building. But the crew had other ideas. 'We fight fires and I don't see any smoke in this building,' said the leading firefighter, as he invited me to climb the ladders to complete what he described as police work.

The other five police officers all looked at me to see what would happen next. I had no choice – it was another put up or shut up time. I started to climb onwards and upwards, but the higher I got the more I wished I was back down on the ground. When I reached the top of the ladders I was hoping to hear a shout from below telling me they had found an alternative way into the building, but it was not to be. I thought that perhaps God was getting his revenge for my interview with the window cleaner. Once I arrived at the top, I could clearly hear the voices coming from the roof. I reckoned there were a number of men on the roof and they sounded as if they were panicking.

Yet the worst part of the climb was still to come. The turntable ladder did not lie tight against the roof; it swayed gently in the air and there was a gap of several inches between it and the building. This meant that I had to swing around the side of the ladder and step over the gap and on to a stone parapet. I was terrified but having come this far, I couldn't just climb back down again.

Once I had braved the gap and was on the roof I still could not see my quarry, although I could hear that they were nearby hidden by the gloom. As I waited for my eyes to acclimatise, I realised that they were likely to be as frightened of me as I had been by the ladders. So, in my deepest challenging voice, I warned them to give themselves up as the place was surrounded by Glasgow's finest and there was a real danger they would fall over the side of the building. Almost immediately they gave themselves up and handed over their bags of swag. A few minutes later I had three young teenagers sitting on the parapet, each with a polythene bag full of jewellery at their feet. I waited for the back-up to arrive but no one else was stupid enough to come up the ladder.

The fire service broke open the doors and, once we had the roof secured, I searched the area as I wasn't convinced all the crooks had been captured. However, I had to call it a day as parts of the roof angled off awkwardly towards internal penned-in areas and I was in danger of falling off.

That morning, a quick stocktake showed we had recovered nearly a quarter of a million pounds worth of jewellery but some was still missing. It left a bad taste in my mouth; after all, each of the teenagers insisted that we had arrested all the crooks and recovered all the stolen property. So where was the missing jewellery?

Later that day, as I tried to catch up on my sleep, I was

woken by a telephone call from an informant. He wanted to know if I had been 'the loony' climbing up the fire brigade ladder on the roof above the jeweller's. He had heard about it in the pub. Apparently it was the talk of the town but he hadn't just called to insult me. He told me that there had been a fourth member of the gang. The crook had been on the roof when I climbed up the ladder but in his haste to escape he had fallen off into one of the penned-in areas and had broken his legs.

According to the informant, the man had lain behind dustbins all night and then, at dawn, had crawled to Argyle Street where he had persuaded a driver to stop and take him to the Royal Infirmary. All I needed to do was go down to the Royal and find the patient brought into the Accident and Emergency Unit at 6am with broken legs. That was no problem; I found my man easily enough but not the stolen jewellery. I also had nothing to link him with the break-in.

By Friday night the doctors had agreed that the man would be freed the next morning and handed into my custody. I took him down to the Stewart Street office where I discovered there was a warrant out for him on another matter. Then I started a series of interviews about the jewellery raid. At first, he was completely intransigent and denied everything. Soon, however, I had proved his alibi was false and also shown his connection with the three others. He realised his position was becoming unsustainable.

Finally on Saturday night, after many hours going back and forth, it became clear that the problem was not so much admitting his involvement but a problem about where the jewellery had been hidden. My strategy in this type of case was to use a series of 'what if' scenarios. The suspect mirrored my approach and explained that his reluctance was because it would drag someone else into the enquiry. After a considerable period of time inching towards each other's position – a bit like a wage negotiation – we arrived at the nub of our problem.

The suspect had indeed been on the roof of Hamilton Laidlaw and had fallen off still holding on to several bags of jewellery. Having crawled away to hide, he had then taken the stolen jewellery with him to the hospital where he had arranged for his mother to pick it up and hide it in a safe place. His mother worked as a cleaner at a well-known newspaper. She had hidden the hoard in the office and our prisoner feared she would be sacked when her employers found out what she had done.

In a case like this, there often comes a moment when an investigator needs to make a leap of faith and trust what the prisoner is saying, and this was just such an occasion. The young man had admitted his involvement in the break-in and told me who had the stolen jewellery. At nearly midnight, I let the prisoner phone his mother and it was agreed she would collect the stolen goods early the next morning when she went into work. She would then meet a police officer near her office, return the missing jewellery and give a statement.

At 7am on the Sunday morning, the mother handed over the stolen jewellery. Her son appeared in court on Monday and later, along with the other accused, was dealt with by the courts. No further action was taken against the mother. She obviously knew the hidden property was stolen but without her co-operation it would never have been recovered. Hamilton Laidlaw had faced a substantial loss but in the end only a few small pieces, lost in the chase over the rooftops, remained unrecovered.

The experience taught me to think twice about seeking help from the fire brigade. I still shiver when I recall that step on to the roof of the building – these things are best left to the firefighters.

21
Taxi – a Fashionable Way to Catch a Crook

Another unusual crime report our CID clerk old Neil passed me concerned a break-in at a building in St Enoch Square. Bob Lauder and I drove down to the square, before getting on with the rest of the day's business.

As usual detective officers have a number of enquiries or investigations to handle at any one time. It is an acquired skill to handle each element of these cases at the right time. If an investigation is left too long, it will lose impetus and the criminal is confident he can avoid being caught. Balancing the many demands of these never-ending reports was always a source of frustration. You wanted to give of your best to everyone but realistically this could rarely be achieved.

Amid such frustrations, this case seemed very unpromising when Bob and I first arrived. Having entered by the narrow front door, we were met by an elderly man who acted, as was very typical at that time, as the elevator 'boy' and the building's caretaker.

This 'boy' was in his seventies and, given he was wearing glasses and a hearing aid, he did not seem likely to be a good witness. My initial impression was confirmed when it came apparent that he knew little about the break-in and could not imagine how it had happened while he was keeping guard on the building.

A substantial amount of valuable women's fashions had been stolen from the fourth-floor office just across from the St Enoch Centre. The staff had received the jackets and dresses that week and were preparing them for display.

The morning of the break-in they had arrived at work to find a panel in the front door had been kicked out and the rooms ransacked. The staff had left the night before at 4.30pm and it soon became clear the break-in had occurred when the building was open – otherwise the main alarm would have been triggered. So it must have happened either first thing in the morning or after 4.30pm the night before.

Given the quantity of goods taken and the fact that the break-in was on the fourth floor, it seemed obvious the thieves must have used the lift. So we headed back down to have a word with our trusty caretaker, who was enjoying a smoke at the front door.

Talking him through the past twenty-four hours, it was clear that the morning had been too busy for anyone to have taken the goods without being noticed. The night before, though, my witness remembered two salesmen had visited the fifth floor and left soon after, carrying boxes. It then struck the caretaker that these well-dressed salesmen were very likely to be our thieves but, even though he shared the lift up and down with them, he could barely remember anything about either of them.

I was just about to give up when I asked our star witness where the men went after leaving the building. They left in a black hackney taxi which was sitting in the square waiting for a hire, he said. Of course, he could not remember the taxi's plate number – who would? However, when I asked the question, he took the wind out my sails by saying he could recall the name of the hackney cab owner that was etched on the side of the taxi.

At first, I wasn't sure I could believe him. After all, here was a man who shared a lift with the suspects and couldn't describe them. When I contacted the Taxi Owners' Association, however, I found the man named had five taxis on the road. TOA contacted the drivers of the five cabs to see if any of them had picked up a fare from St Enoch Square the previous afternoon.

To my surprise, a few hours later a taxi driver called at Stewart Street police office and told me he had been hired by two travelling salesmen and had taken them to a house in the Rutherglen area of the city. He agreed to take us to the same house straight away.

Bob Lauder and I followed the taxi driver who pointed us to a block of flats about eight miles from the city centre. We started to search the tenement but without success. As we approached the final house, I began to wonder if I had pushed my luck too far. Had the thieves just walked through the tenement block to a nearby house? My doubts increased when an attractive woman answered the final door and told me confidently that I had come to the wrong house. Her demeanour changed when we insisted on having a look round as it would only be fair as we had already checked all the other flats.

At first she tried to say I was being unreasonable but when she realised that we were not going away, somewhat reluctantly she let us into her home. She followed me as I walked around the beautifully appointed flat. When I opened the master bedroom I saw dresses and gowns hanging off every available shelf and covering the double bed and furniture.

I gasped audibly but the woman looked me in the eye and insisted she had never seen these dresses before. This was just ridiculous. Soon her husband turned up, arriving from the shop which they ran together. He was furious with her for letting us in without a warrant and soon they were both facing prosecution for resetting stolen property.

For me and Bob, it was all in a day's work. An unlikely

witness and a taxi driver had led us to the criminals. Another result but, best of all, the goods were returned to their owners who had presumed they were lost forever.

22

Gambling with the Chinese Triads

Being an effective police officer is about much more than simply responding to the call and appeals from the public; a good investigator needs to put himself about and get a feel for what's coming up in his area. It's not unlike networking in commercial business where firms make sure they are prepared for new opportunities which may develop.

So a good detective officer will have contacts with people in his area who, though not involved in criminality, are likely to have an awareness of criminals.

Back in the 1970s police officers were discouraged from going into casinos. The security people were uneasy if the police, even plainclothes officers, turned up at their establishments. Because the police were so unwelcome at the casinos, the criminals moved in and frequented these clubs where they were able to meet and do business in peace.

By late 1978, I had decided this was no longer acceptable and applied for membership of all the Glasgow casinos using the address of Stewart Street police office. I was surprised when my memberships arrived without question and I was now the proud member of every casino in town. My membership also allowed me to sign in a friend – which of course was whoever I was on duty with that evening.

At first, the security staff were not comfortable with my

regular visits but soon they were used to me popping in for a cup of coffee, seeing the sights, and moving on. After some months, I began to get to know the casino managers and soon became aware of the problems facing them and the people causing them concern.

George Themis, then manager of the Regency Casino, became a good friend at this time. George, a Greek Cypriot who had come to Scotland to work for the Stakis Group, had a wide knowledge of gambling and the people who hung about casinos. He helped me understand the clubs where the very rich could lose thousands in a night without the slightest concern and, at the other end of the scale, clubs where the unemployed would gamble their last £10 in the hope of doubling their cash.

With the hospitality of free coffee and sandwiches, and even free meals for select customers, such casinos were an extremely comfortable environment for criminals to gather unchallenged at little expense.

George, who died in the 1980s, helped me to gain a privileged view of this world. I have never understood the allure of gaming but I could see its attraction to criminals with its easy come, easy go approach.

There were high standards at the casinos. In the Chevalier Casino, in the suitably named Hope Street, the gamblers were all required to wear a suit, collar and tie. Most of the senior managers were Greek Cypriots or locals who had been with the company for a considerable time. There was a particular glamour to these clubs with young, attractive female staff dressed in long, flowing evening dresses and high heels which contrasted sharply with the drab city life outside.

George and his colleagues took great pride in their businesses and ensured that the casinos were well run. Drunkenness and violence were extremely rare. However, I could see that many of the so-called gang figures enjoyed the hospitality of the Chevalier.

A second casino, the Regent, was just around the corner and provided for a more working-class clientele. Here I saw, amongst others, large numbers of Chinese and Asian workers gambling their wages away.

During this time I was eventually shown behind the scenes to a secret closed-circuit television monitoring centre that the casinos operated. These days films such as *Ocean's Eleven* have revealed how the casinos monitor the gambling tables, but back in the 1970s little was known about their secret facilities. When I saw the operation for the first time, I was hugely impressed.

These facilities were to prove a huge advantage to the police. I was able to see if a criminal group were in a club without going into the casino itself. The tapes were also to prove valuable when checking alibis or associations between criminals, though rules for access had to be agreed to ensure civil liberty issues were properly addressed.

It was a casual conversation at one of these casinos that sparked off the first Triad-related investigation in Scotland. George told me and Willie Williamson, a colleague from Stewart Street CID, that his Chinese customers appeared ill at ease and occasionally frightened in the presence of a particular group of young Chinese men. George, unusually, did not know these men but he had found them highly demanding and slightly intimidating in their manner. He had also noticed that some of his best customers left the casino when they saw this group of men appear and he had been told by his customers that they were members of a Triad.

Willie and I spent the next year visiting Chinese families. During the day we dealt with our normal duties and at night we went to meet Chinese businessmen in their restaurants or homes to try to find out what caused them to live in fear of this group.

A year later, in August of 1979, we were to identify and convict the leader of the group, Chan King Wing. This twenty-seven-year-old man claimed to be working as a waiter but, throughout our investigations, he never worked a single day. This didn't, however, stop him living the high life. By then, Willie and I had become experts on the Triads. We were also to take statements from more than thirty Chinese witnesses in Inverness, Aberdeen, Dundee, Edinburgh and Glasgow.

Initially, the investigation was extremely difficult. Although there had been a Chinese community in Scotland since the 1950s, they had always kept themselves to themselves. Willie and I started interviewing possible witnesses and we were viewed with suspicion when we visited restaurant owners and their staff; they preferred to divert us with small talk and a coffee or a meal. The Chinese kept telling us they didn't know of any gangs in Scotland threatening Chinese families and they also made it plain that, if such groups did exist, the police wouldn't be able to help them.

After several weeks of frustration, information started to trickle in. At first it was an anonymous written note or phone call. Because of the strong Chinese accents, we often struggled to make out what these phone messages said. At one stage even Sir David McNee, then the Commissioner of the Metropolitan Police, received a letter from 'The Peaceful Citizen' suggesting that Chinese Triads were operating in Glasgow. Around this time, a *Daily Record* reporter was also told by a Chinese businessman that Triads were operating in Scotland.

Our colleagues back in Stewart Street watched all these developments with much interest. They were influenced by the fact that the Chinese don't talk to the police. Across Europe it had certainly been the case that Chinese communities affected by Triad activities refused to speak to the authorities. I was determined, however, that this would not happen in Scotland.

Throughout our rounds of interviews, Willie and I had been impressed by the Chinese community with their hard-working ethos and the obvious pride they took in their families. However, it was clear that many of our Chinese 'friends' were frightened and were being intimidated. Breaking down this wall of silence was proving to be very difficult.

Willie had been in the Merchant Navy before joining the police and had some experience of the Chinese and their culture but I knew very little about them. Through Interpol, I was put in a touch with a Triad expert based in Paris. I learned from him how the Triads operated through threats of violence towards family and businesses. Chinese men also feared a public 'loss of face' to a Triad member. This would usually occur at a Chinese event or function, where a respected member of the community would be assaulted or forced to give way to the Triad boss. Triad members would thereafter visit businesses and 'invite' the owners to lend *Tai Ko* (meaning the One who has Power or 'Big Brother' – the term used to describe a Triad boss) a specified sum of money. The sum could be sizeable and there would then follow regular demands for cash. Once it was clear the demands had come from a Triad boss, most businessmen found the demands very difficult to refuse.

Chan King Wing followed this description almost to the book. To demonstrate his power, Chan confronted one of Glasgow's most respected businessmen publicly and demanded more than £5,000. When the businessman refused, Chan slapped him across the face in front of the Chinese community. The effect was electric. It sent a bolt of fear through those present and thereafter to the wider Chinese community when they heard about it. They were gripped by fear not just for their own safety but also for their families back home in Hong Kong and China.

23
The Courage of a Lion

After the confrontation at a Chinese restaurant in Glasgow city centre, Chan King Wing was identified by the Chinese community as a *Tai Ko*. He was an all-powerful boss of a Triad group known as Soi Fong, which along with 14K and Wo Shing Wo are Triad groups known to operate across the world.

Soi Fong, or Water Room, was thought to have been created by prisoners in the Far East who had worked together in a Chinese jail laundry room. They had created their powerful gang to compete with other criminal groups to extort money and organise crime across the world. Soi Fong had proved extremely effective and it controlled with a culture of fear and intimidation. From a standing start in Scotland in 1978, Chan King Wing created an organisation capable of frightening the whole of the Chinese community.

Willie and I spent long hours, over many months, sitting in restaurants or at the casinos spending time with restaurateurs and their staff, winkling out evidence. As is often the way, witnesses were happy to tell us what was happening to other members of their community but not to talk about themselves. From this third-party reporting we managed to build up a picture of what was going on across Scotland.

Willie and I knew that the criminal gang demanded what they called 'lucky money' for their boss, who was identified as Chan. The sums were always unusual – £1,080, £10,180 or similar – and were identifiable as being lucky numbers. These demands were accompanied by threats of rape, assaults or the abduction of children.

After a long time our hard work paid off as we began to get witnesses willing to speak directly to us. Even so, every person implored us not to reveal their existence as a witness, even to their nearest friends. I told them that they would have to be identified eventually when it came to identification parades and a court case.

Throughout our investigation, our quarry appeared completely ignorant of what we were up to. Had he been part of a Scottish gang, there is little doubt in my mind he would have realised we were on his trail. It was therefore a complete shock to Chan King Wing and his five lieutenants when we arrested him one afternoon as he made one of his usual visits to a Glasgow casino. Despite claiming to be out of work, he and his associates were dressed up to the nines in expensive, fashionable clothes.

The arrest led to more problems. The gang now insisted they could only speak in a Hakka dialect of Chinese despite their obvious ability to converse with Chinese groups across Scotland. Such was the fear of reprisals that innocent Chinese men refused to take part as stand-ins in identification parades and we were forced to run an identification parade made up only of accused people.

Les Brown, who was then a Detective Inspector, was in charge of the parade to be held at Stewart Street police office in Glasgow. Les had a wide experience and knowledge of the criminal underworld across the city. He had been involved in a whole series of significant arrests and was a well-respected detective officer. He had seen it all in his time so I was curious when he sent for me before the parade began. It turned out that a witness had arrived in a police car in a lion's costume, complete with a lion's head. The witness was standing at the front desk, refusing to confirm his name to the officers there and was insisting on seeing me.

I was soon able to identify the lion as a local Chinese businessman. He was so terrified of the prospect of facing his tormentors that he had hired the costume. He said that as well as protecting his identity, the lion's outfit would give him the courage he needed to identify the suspects.

As it happened, this parade was one of the first in Scotland to use a one-way mirror to enable a witness to view a parade of possible suspects without being seen. Although each of the Chinese witnesses had been told about the mirror, it wasn't until the lion witness actually saw the arrangement that he agreed to take part in the parade without his headgear, allowing the parade manager, Les Brown, to properly identify him as a witness. Later the case of the lion witness was to provide much hilarity during the trial at the High Court.

Knowing all of the witnesses, I realised how much fear and anxiety they suffered taking part in the parade. I also felt that it was terrible that a respectable, educated family man had been driven to such lengths to dress up in a costume to perform his civic duty.

The trial at the High Court proved particularly challenging for all concerned. Each of the accused needed to have an interpreter and every statement had to be translated between Chinese and English. Progress was tortuously slow. So it was no surprise that, after only a few of the witnesses had given evidence, Chan King Wing offered a plea and his co-accused offered not guilty pleas.

At the end of the case Lord Robertson said: 'It is the duty of this court to reassure the law-abiding Chinese community in Scotland that this sort of conduct, threats by self-styled powerful men and the like, will not be tolerated here.'

Chan King Wing was sentenced to five years.

This was not the last time I saw Chan. When he was

released, I went to see him to return his property as he was being deported to Hong Kong. Chan was surprised when I returned his money to him – he thought I would just have kept it for myself! By this time he displayed a good understanding of English which he had mastered in prison.

As he set off in his by now less than fashionable suit, I wondered how long it would be before we saw further similar attacks on the Chinese community.

In 1985, Philip Wong, a well-known Glasgow businessman and someone who had been a witness in our case, was leaving a Chinese community shop when he was set upon by a group of young Chinese men. Philip was attacked ferociously with cleavers and knives. His murder had all the hallmarks of a Triad execution but I'll deal with this a little later.

Today, the Chinese community in Scotland, alongside the Vietnamese community, have been used as a cover for criminals investing in the industrial cultivation of cannabis or 'grows' as they have become known across the world. This development was first uncovered in Australia, Canada and the USA before being discovered in the UK. Run by organised crime, it provides substantial profits to the gangs. I have no doubt some of those profits in these circumstances will end up in Triad organisations who will invest their profits in other lucrative forms of criminal activity.

24
My Very Small Role
in *Taggart*

Late in 1982, I was approached by Andy Stewart, a Central CID detective nicknamed the Scottish Soldier, to speak to an actor who was about to play a Glasgow detective on television. The actor, Mark McManus, was keen to meet some police officers and talk about their work. At the time I was working with the Serious Crime Squad and I was reluctant to meet him, but I was told Mark was particularly keen to see me.

When we met up at the Heilandman's Umbrella at Argyle Street one lunchtime, he turned up dressed in the same type of suit and Burberry coat as me. He had obviously done his homework and even had his scarf worn to show his collar and tie, as was so typical of police officers at that time. I pulled his leg about it as we went off for a bite of lunch.

It soon became clear that Mark was determined to make his character as realistic as possible and was very keen to hear examples of interviews and incidents I had been involved in. He had already spoken to a number of detective officers in the city and it was obvious that Mark was very enthusiastic and I warmed to him. When I left him and wished him well, little did I realise how good his new role would turn out to be.

Later, when I was appointed a Chief Inspector at Saracen police office, I wanted to prove my worth to the area. Much of the action in *Taggart* is set around the Saracen and Maryhill areas of Glasgow and I thought Mark could help with an Open Day at the police office. There had been Open Days across the force for a number of years but it wasn't thought to be a good idea in Saracen, a tough inner-city area. I disagreed.

Many of the young men from the area had spent time in the Saracen police cells and I thought it was important to open the office to dispel the rumours and lies that had been spread about what the cells were like and what the police got up to in the office.

By this time, Mark was a big TV star because of his huge success in *Taggart*. When I contacted him, Mark said he would be delighted to turn up and help. Early in 1988, the officers at Saracen had prepared the Open Day for a Saturday. Local politicians and community leaders came to show their support for the police and Mark and his partner turned out as promised for the 10am opening, although I was getting extremely worried because they turned up at the very last moment. I had feared that local people wouldn't be interested, but as soon as Mark arrived people poured into the office to see him.

I had expected Mark to stay for an hour or so but he stayed all day, taking time to speak to the crowds queuing to see the various displays and speaking to staff. Mark was fabulous and he had the locals eating out of his hands. Taggart really had taken over Saracen CID for the day. There might have been a 'murrda' somewhere in the city that day but in Saracen everyone was enjoying a great day out.

At one point, one of our regular lock-ups took his two children into the cells to show them the spartan conditions. He warned them that, if they were as stupid as him, they would also end up in the cells and he did not want that to

146

happen. This, for me, is what Open Days at a police office are really all about.

When Mark left at 5 o'clock it was clear that he had enjoyed the day every bit as much as the locals and as he left he promised that, should I need anything else, he would be happy to help again.

Some months later when I got in touch about making an educational video looking into drugs and the impact of peer pressure upon youngsters, Mark was again happy to help. He also encouraged some actors to come to Possilpark for the day where, with Seargent Ronnie Collins, the Saracen Crime Prevention Officer, they produced *Taggart's Team* – a twenty minute video looking at situations youngsters find themselves in that can lead to substance abuse.

None of Mark's team of actors took a penny for their time, so the financial support we obtained from the Variety Club was spent exclusively on producing the video and teaching packages. Looking back, I now realise that Taggart's Team was a precursor for the *Choices for Life* education packages that we developed and produced for youngsters in the 1990s.

I spoke to Mark a few times in the period leading up to his untimely death. It was clear that he had been unwell and he became worse after his wife died. Nothing could have kept me away from his funeral and the turnout was overwhelming. Mark deserved nothing less, he gave of his time unselfishly, particularly for young people across Scotland.

After the success at Saracen, I later held similar Open Days in Hamilton and Airdrie. Every time locals turned out in their droves, keen to see what really happens inside the police station. At Airdrie, I organised a Christmas party for needy local kids, as I had at Saracen. The party at Airdrie was particularly successful, thanks to two people: Maurice Johnston and Vera Weisfeld.

What Every Woman Wants, owned by Vera's family,

allowed me to choose thousands of pounds' worth of presents for the children at no cost. They were incredibly generous and demanded nothing in return and didn't seek any publicity for the extraordinary gift. It was a privilege to be a part of being able to help these children and the impact of this generosity cannot be overstated.

I had wanted rank-and-file officers and staff to be reminded of the caring part of police work. All too often, police are caught in the corrosive experience of being so close to abuse and violence. It is easy to forget how difficult life can be for many disadvantaged people in our communities.

I also wanted to open up links between police officers and members of our local communities. I hoped that by being involved in these events, particularly within some of the most challenging housing estates, we might create relationships which in the future would prevent street violence, would stop police officers from being hurt and, at the same time, give disadvantaged kids the chance to see a future for themselves.

Not being a football fan, I didn't know what to expect when it was suggested to me that Mo Johnston would make a good guest at our Christmas party. He had something of an unfortunate reputation in Glasgow, having played for both Rangers and Celtic. He was also known to have some questionable characters as friends. Nonetheless, Mo was a treat to deal with.

When I asked the police office staff who the visiting children would most like to see at the Christmas lunch, Mo was their favourite. When I sent a message to him, this young and surprisingly shy man called me within a week asking what he could do to help. He took little persuading to come along to the Christmas party.

Mo had agreed to turn up at Airdrie police office by 2pm on the Sunday afternoon to kick off the party. There was mayhem at the police station as the staff had arranged for

150 children to join in. Police and staff, who throughout the year had complained about the incivility and hostility of the locals, rolled up their sleeves and mucked in. It was a huge operation planning food, soft drinks, decorations and presents as well as a DJ and decorations to make the hall look festive.

Mo and his partner turned up with their newborn child in plenty of time but he seemed very nervous. He became even more jumpy when I told him I wanted him to dress up as Santa Claus and hand out all the presents. By then, we realised that we had more children than presents but Vera came up trumps once again, authorising staff to donate another twenty presents from her Airdrie shop.

By 3pm, the party was in full swing and Santa received the biggest cheer as he went around handing out the presents. One hour later, when Mo took off his beard, the kids went wild yet again. After half an hour, dozens of kids were outside in the yard playing football with their idol. Mo's earlier nervousness had been overcome and he eventually had to be persuaded to leave.

The smiles on the faces of the staff showed me that the day was as worthwhile for the police and office staff as it had been for the locals. The party also reminded us that the police are a public service and we are not just out to arrest criminals – we are also there to support those least able to look after themselves in our difficult and divided world.

25
What Makes a
Good Criminal

Many of my informants, or 'touts' as they are better known, have told me that they had really wanted to be police officers. I was often struck by the way these touts would think and behave just like us. This often meant that I'd receive good quality information that led to vital evidence needed to secure a conviction at court. Touts rarely provided useless information.

In many ways the very skills that make a successful criminal are evident in a good detective; both live by a set of rules and conventions designed to protect them. For street criminals, the first rule is never to 'grass' but that would be better rewritten as 'never get caught informing'. There are very few criminals I can recall who refused to deal with a police officer, under the right circumstances. Criminals, just like a good detective officer, seek to be invisible when out and about on the streets. Whether out scouting for a crime, or just assessing criminal opportunities, a thief never wants to be noticed.

So, criminals out on the streets will always try to protect themselves from the possibility of identification or, even worse, arrest. They are constantly watching out for the police, security staff or nosey members of the public who may be a witness against them at court. A thief will always go out of his way to dress, behave and conduct himself in a way that appears normal.

The criminal, however, draws attention from the watchers who are looking out for something unusual because creating the appearance of being normal takes a good deal of effort. Such criminals are more likely to be noticed because they are either constantly watching out for trouble without moving their head or they are on the move and walking too fast because they are nervous, having just committed a crime.

Trying to dress the part, a criminal will often appear out of place by overlooking part of the costume, either from a lack of knowledge or an inability to carry through the act. In many respects, plainclothes officers do exactly the same thing. When trying to dress in street clothes, police officers often end up looking alike, wearing denims, T-shirts and trainers.

Police officers also want to make sure they can see everything that's happening on the street around them but they don't have the natural reserve of the criminal who fears imminent arrest. This can leave officers looking like swivel heads, constantly on the lookout for a thief but in reality giving themselves away to the criminals they want to catch.

Criminals have come to expect identikit police officers: two white men wearing 'street' clothes and jackets designed to hide their police radio and other equipment. This is just one the many reasons that it's essential to ensure that police forces recruit more women and increasing numbers of people from ethnic minorities for this type of work. Criminals effectively ignore the threat from women and people from ethnic minorities because they are so confident that they won't be police officers.

Investigators who are out on the street need to become part of the street life and need to watch all round them so that they become a part of the culture. They can only do this if they know what behaviour is normal and what will raise suspicion, allowing a criminal the chance to escape. Indecision is a police officer's worst enemy.

As a nineteen-year-old officer I started to people-watch, just looking on as ordinary people went about their legitimate business. When off-duty, out shopping or with nothing better to do, I would watch the world going by from a street corner, simply noting how people behaved as they passed by. At first, I found it hard to concentrate as my mind would wander and I was incapable of seeing anything out of the ordinary. It is essential to notice any changes in the landscape but seeing these and understanding why they have happened is the key to spotting criminals.

Immense patience is needed – criminals will always operate at their own pace. You could say that a good detective is like being a good fisherman – he casts out his line at the part of the river most likely to attract a good catch and then has to just wait patiently.

Understanding what is usual on the street gives the police officer both the experience to make a judgement about what isn't right and the confidence to act on his or her instinct. It might be the body language that appears to be wrong. People are usually too preoccupied with their own business to notice much that is happening around them. They appear relaxed and carry things with no sense of self-awareness. A thief, on the other hand, is desperate to know exactly what is happening around him and will immerse himself into the scene. He will make eye contact with everyone close to him, checking them all out.

A criminal creates a ten-metre exclusion zone around himself to ensure that a police officer can never get close enough to intercept and arrest him. If a criminal thinks he has spotted a police officer his face changes. The eyes widen and the jaw tightens in shock at the prospect of what is about to happen. However, a thief is preoccupied at the moment of committing a crime – at that moment he becomes blinded as he is mesmerized by his 'target' and becomes vulnerable.

A good officer will be able to spot what makes the thief stand out. It may be a piece of clothing that doesn't quite fit or match up. Sometimes the criminal will be extremely well dressed but something is not quite right – perhaps a too-cheap or too-expensive coat that looks out of place or badly worn or marked shoes that don't match the rest of the outfit. Sometimes it can be a shirt and tie that don't fit in and might be either dirty or in a contrasting style. In other cases it may be a piece of bling or a fake suntan that makes the whole look overdone and just shouts 'crook'!

Some professional criminals dress up in overalls or workwear, so that they can wander into storerooms or shop areas unchallenged. However, under that clothing they may be wearing the 'wrong' look of suit or have soft hands, unusual tattoos, or jewellery that gives them away.

Often it was poorly kept shoes that gave away a thief and led me to notice something else was out of place. Criminals would probably say that many a pair of well-polished shoes have given away the presence of a police officer, although the switch to wearing trainers has changed that.

An effective police officer will be able to tell the difference between a suspect and a member of the public who just is a little bit different or eccentric in some way. Surveillance can often clear up any doubts without a person even realising they are a suspect. On a bad day, a suspect taking to his heels can, of course, confirm a suspicion but a police officer who knows his streets and criminals can usually avoid such an outcome.

At the moment of arrest, a police officer has a split second to take control of the situation. This can be a difficult balancing act. If you are too tough and are mistaken then you can end up with egg on your face and a complaint. If you are too soft then the criminal can flee, leaving you with egg on your face yet again.

Detectives, therefore, also need to have a good memory for faces, names and associations between people. Access to criminal records and photographs can give the police officer the upper hand when recognising a criminal before he has the chance to realise that you are a police officer.

Watching criminals and knowing who they are and where they meet can help a detective build up their own profile of a crook. Knowing their preferred meeting places enables an officer to hang about the area unseen and build up a picture of their habits and routines. Knowing the links between crooks can also prove invaluable when you need to trace someone in a hurry.

During an interview, it can be of immense value to introduce such knowledge, without saying how you came to know it. Criminals always assume that someone has 'grassed' them up. The last thing a criminal will think is that a police officer has actually done his homework.

The successful detective will be that officer who links street observations to the information he gathers from touts and intelligence. The bringing together of these skills produces a powerful weapon against crime.

26
A University Education

My first thirteen years in the police service had introduced me quickly to the realities of crime on Scotland's streets. I had gone from an inexperienced nineteen-year-old Glasgow youth to a well-respected detective, who was called on regularly to help in a wide range of investigations.

It was a time of great change throughout the world, particularly the criminal world. The commission of crime was becoming more complex just as armed robbery, housebreaking and car theft became difficult. At the same time the courts demanded, quite rightly, a planned approach to evidence-gathering rather than the somewhat haphazard methods the police had used previously.

It was also becoming more difficult for me personally, as more and more criminals knew me and could recognise me. I was no longer able to walk the streets unnoticed by criminals, which meant I had lost the element of surprise.

I felt it was time for me to look for new ideas and challenges. I was delighted, therefore, to be accepted as a full-time police-sponsored student at the University of Glasgow. I was to spend the next three years at the university I had so often passed as a child but always thought would never be open to people from my background.

As a serving police inspector, I was given the time to consider the future issues affecting the service, while completing a Master of Arts degree. It gave me the chance to think through some of the big issues that had given me concern since I had first joined the police service. How can we seek to offer genuine security to everyone in our community and not just to rich and influential people? What arrangements should modern-day Scotland make to ensure its police forces remain accountable in an effective way to our communities?

Throughout my time as a student, I maintained day-to-day contact with investigations to make sure I kept up to date with the changes. Like other police students, I returned to work with the police during the holidays but, quite properly, I was allocated administrative duties rather than the frontline policing I enjoyed so much. I still continued to receive information about criminals which helped ensure stolen property was recovered, drugs seized and wanted people were arrested.

One spring night in 1985, I was phoned by a member of the Chinese community, who was in a terrible panic, telling me that Philip Wong, a well-known and respected member of their community, had been killed by a group of Triad men in the street in Glasgow's Garnethill area. I rang police headquarters to be told that officers were on their way to investigate a reported attack in Renfrew Street.

Philip had been ambushed as he was walking to his car after coming out of a shop. He was attacked by a group of men and hacked to death. I knew Philip and his family well; he was an experienced and respected businessman.

He had been a witness in the Chan King Wing Triad case I had investigated a few years earlier but his evidence hadn't been vital to that case. Nevertheless, given what I knew about the Chinese culture and Triad traditions, I was very concerned. I spoke about my fears to the enquiry team early that morning. A number of men from the Chinese community also contacted me to tell what had been going on and I was relieved to be told that a recent event had led to the killing and my case played no part in Philip's murder. I was told that the cause of this crime lay in a business disagreement that had affected Triad interests.

I was deeply saddened that a married man with three children could be slaughtered on the streets of Scotland in this way. It has been alleged that the Triad group Woo Sang Wu were behind Philip's murder over attempts to extort profits from his lucrative video tape hire business. It was chilling to realise that members of this Triad group were relatively new to Scotland and were competing alongside the 14K and Soi Fong groups traditionally known to have influence across the country. If intelligence at the time was accurate, the bold nature of Philip's murder demonstrates clearly the callous and casual way murder is treated by such organised crime groups and why they are so dangerous to Scotland. What is certainly true is that the people thought to be involved in this appalling murder left the United Kingdom very quickly to take advantage of the jungle of international laws which would allow them to hide from their responsibilities.

In the modern world, such crimes should be resolved before a criminal court. Today, the presence of Asian crime groups is recognised as being behind the rising problem of cannabis cultivations affecting all of Scotland. Chinese finance and support provide the environment for Vietnamese 'gardeners' to be brought illegally into the country to maintain the cultivations or 'grows' of cannabis skunk for gang profits. At the same time Chinese criminals organise the door-to-door delivery of counterfeit DVD films, pornography and tobacco around Scottish communities. Again there is little doubt Triad groups benefit from these businesses and they use poor migrant workers to sell product. The profits are passed through a series of layered banking arrangements to benefit gang bosses. Even in the spring of 2008, I witnessed young Chinese men going door-to-door around businesses in Glasgow selling pornographic DVDs and Hollywood films. The lucrative profits are siphoned off for the benefit of organised crime groups often based elsewhere in the world.

It was at the time of Philip Wong's murder that I decided to study the transnational effect of organised criminality. Whilst it was easy to understand the problems investigators faced trying to bring criminals who had fled a country to justice, I wanted to understand how organised crime took advantage of national borders to protect their businesses. The *French Connection* story demonstrated clearly how European and American criminals worked together to avoid arrest whilst importing heroin to America from France. I therefore decided to visit the New York Police Department as part of a Churchill Scholarship for Scotland award to learn more about their approach to organised and serious crime but more of that elsewhere.

My university studies changed the course of my career. When I returned to Strathclyde Police, I was appointed a uniformed officer, first as an Inspector on a shift and later as a Chief Inspector. Although I failed to appreciate it at the time, I realised later that this change was one of the best things that could have happened to me. It reminded me of my broader police responsibilities and brought me back into contact with the general public. I had probably spent too much time dealing with criminals, their crimes and conspiracies than was good for me.

I had been developing a jaundiced view of the world, full as it had been with robbers, murderers and con men. Back in uniform, I soon realised that there were still many decent people who needed police support at very challenging moments in their lives. Whether it was cases of domestic abuse, suicides or road accidents, the presence of police officers, who care and try to help, could bring enormous comfort and support to families when they needed it most.

During this time, I became increasingly aware of the challenge police faced trying to make ends meet with resources that are patently insufficient to cope. The liberalisation of our drinking culture, the widening of access to nightlife, together with our young generation's experiences of clubs in places such as Majorca and Ibiza, brought a new acceptance of a drug culture to Scotland. At the same time, the growing and understandable demand from police staff that they should have a work-life balance, additional days off and holidays in line with other workers, meant that, as round-the-clock demands for the police grew, the number of officers available for work shrunk.

My experience as a beat officer, walking a relatively quiet night shift street often occupied solely by cops and robbers, had disappeared. Today, some of our main streets are busier at three in the morning than they are at three in the afternoon.

In the light of growing bureaucratic demands, imposed by administrators in the belief that performance measurement and management was the means to deliver a more effective and efficient service, few of the real issues affecting the public were grasped. Some senior officers who had merely a passing understanding of the service thought measurement was the key to success. This approach generated a greater need for record keeping and bureaucracy at the very time the public was demanding a more personalised service with an increased presence on the streets. This created the absurd situation where the demands continued to grow whilst availability of officers slumped due to training and administrative duties. The shortening of the working week and increased holidays have merely exacerbated the problem.

There is also a commonly repeated mantra which goes: 'it's not more staff we need, it's better IT'. I could never understand this. Administrators, happy with their nine-to-five existence, dictate what will work in the real world. They, however, have never faced the reality of the sudden demand for police officers or the need for the specialist skills of a particular staff member who has just finished a sixteen-hour shift. Just like Bill Shankly's famous quote about football, policing isn't about life and death, it's more important than that. What we really require is more staff *and* better IT.

In the housing estates around the country, there are many families living on the edge who owe their peace and tranquillity to the support and activity of their local police. Equally, there are even more families who don't have that support and, as a result, live solitary and isolated lives. They are forced to remain indoors and out of sight of their local tormentors, who are frequently the estate's youths or local drunks.

It is the responsibility of any fair society to ensure that all of our citizens are able to go about their business unfettered. The provision of properly trained officers on the streets would act not just as a deterrent but could also prevent situations escalating to the level where arrest and imprisonment are required.

Alongside this, we must ensure educational and job opportunities for those less able to achieve qualifications. It is no surprise that the majority of people in our prisons today have literacy and numeracy problems and were excluded or absent from school from an early age. In the police, we used to call that a clue. On the basis of such clues, there is some basic but hard and unattractive work to be done to make sure these young people have a future. Goodness knows, we have a dearth of plumbers, joiners and builders in Scotland.

Instead of tackling these issues head on, we now have fewer interventions at street level but more bureaucracy and reporting. Today's police are burdened with immense paperwork associated with even the simplest of prosecutions. The possibility of Legal Aid means there can be trials for almost all accused and, in addition, there are the burdens of sex offender monitoring, risk assessments, international terrorism and increasing numbers of public events such as pop concerts and extra football matches. These many and varied conflicting demands make it extremely difficult to prioritise policing resources effectively, but that does not stop politicians and the public demanding that their particular need receives attention, without recognising the overall impact.

Meanwhile, accused men (it is usually men who transgress) come to believe that their actions are neither their responsibility nor morally wrong. From their view, if their actions were illegal or reprehensible, then surely the authorities would focus attention on the crimes, not the paperwork. In reality, more time is spent dealing with paperwork, and the provision Legal Aid or bail, than is spent dealing with the actual crime and its victim. Given all this, it is easy to understand current police frustrations.

Attempts to fill this void by creating new members of the 'police family' are a false economy and short-sighted in my view. It is unfair to both the community patrols and the public to send people out on to the streets without the ability to arrest an offender. If we need extra patrols, we should train and appoint constables.

Personal safety and security is the foundation stone of any democracy. If our families and our properties cannot be kept safe, we will return to the era of lawlessness and the survival of the fittest. Every day, many of the poorest and weakest in our community face the prospect of living with that helplessness. It is not acceptable that people in the United Kingdom, one of the world's most affluent societies, should suffer in this way.

The police service, for its part, must demonstrate its ability to deliver effectively if staff numbers are increased. Administrative and support functions must be identified and civilianised to ensure that police officers are utilised solely in jobs demanding policing skills. In 1986, I briefed a senior politician about the need to resource the police service properly to improve the lives of ordinary people. It took until after 2000, and only after some horse trading in the Scottish Parliament, for there to be any real commitment to increase the numbers of police officers significantly.

Officers' conditions of service probably need to be re-examined to make sure that the public are clear about what the police are there for and to ensure that they're happy to pay for this effective support. Meantime, there must be improvements in the service to reflect any additional resources spent.

In New York, significant increases in police officers on the beat transformed the city's prospects. The city, which had thousands of murders, was on the verge of bankruptcy during the 1980s. Today, the investment in policing has been repaid many times over as it is now a relatively safe and welcoming place for tourists. New York once again leads the world in terms of affluence and economic growth and effective and well-resourced policing has played a key role in this revival.

27
NYPD, Washington
and the FBI

In the early 1980s, I was fortunate to have the chance to spread my wings and travel abroad to see how other countries were policed. These were years of development for me and I studied at the University of Glasgow as a police-sponsored student. I was keen to travel to America and, financed by the Churchill Memorial Trust for Scotland, I arranged a secondment to One Police Plaza, in the New York Police Department.

When I reported for duty in June 1985 in New York, having made sure before I left that my trip had been confirmed, the police headquarters appeared to know nothing about it. It became apparent to me that the administration within the office was fairly chaotic and that the staff had made little preparation for my arrival. In fairness, it was also evident that the NYPD were sometimes overcome with the sheer numbers of visitors who sought to learn from them. In the circumstances a Scottish police inspector was hardly a priority. I was asked to give them a week to sort out the situation.

I had spent my first weekend in the city walking around the area of my hotel, a YMCA just north of 42nd Street, and the area summed up the terrible problems afflicting New York at that time. The streets were strewn with litter and the terrible effects of drug abuse were evident. The fear generated by the little understood HIV/AIDS epidemic afflicting the gay community was at its height. The newspaper headlines reflected a city living in fear of AIDS and crime in equal measure. The city was increasingly being abandoned by big business and its workers who were moving to new and safer places across America. As a result, the economy was faltering and public services were beginning to fail due to lack of funding.

My first impressions of the city's police were equally unfavourable. The few police found on the streets were scruffy and I had been warned by the hotel staff not to approach them. In spite of an early intimation from my own Chief Constable, my arrival at police headquarters just confirmed my depressing initial impression. Having being met with little enthusiasm from officers at the Commissioner's office, I discovered that the Manhattan South Precinct was reputed to be the busiest police office in the world. That was the place for me and I made my way there to introduce myself. Luckily, I was seconded to a great team of detectives who took me under their wing.

New York was facing meltdown. The finances were so chaotic that, every month, the force struggled to organise enough cash to pay the monthly wage bill. Recruitment was also problematic and the Commissioner, in a move extremely unpopular with rank-and-file officers, had recently merged the New York Transit Authority Police with the NYPD.

There were a record number of homicides, with more than 2,000 murders each year in New York. Crack cocaine and heroin were easily available and areas around the projects – public housing – and districts such as Harlem had a fearful reputation. Recently, when I saw the movie *American Gangster*, with Denzel Washington, I was struck by how well it captured the atmosphere of the streets of New York as they were during my brief time there.

I found it very strange that many of the detectives I met, as well as working for the police, also ran their own security companies or took on private contracts when off-duty. Arrangements were acceptable to the police department and were subject of routine authorisation. I couldn't see how police officers could reconcile such conflicts of interest in their minds. It seemed to me that often their police duties were merely an opportunity to make a business contact for the future.

Despite all these disappointments, I met some first-class officers who worked tirelessly on behalf of the city. Jerry McQueen was one such officer. Jerry, who was a senior detective at one of the precincts, made sure I got a real insight into organised crime in the city and what it was like to deal with organised crime groups, such as the Mafia, and the newly formed migrant gangs, particularly the Russians.

In 1985, a typical murder in New York City was investigated by two detectives for about three days. If there were no leads then the enquiry was put in a live file, where it would remain until some new evidence was uncovered. As a result the homicide detection level was unbelievably low. Indeed, American officers found it hard to believe the resources normally committed to a murder investigation in Scotland. Given the huge number of murders they experienced this was not very surprising.

There were few computers in evidence across the precincts and most detectives still filed reports on paper, giving up the opportunity to cross-reference investigations. This seemed incredible to me. There were large numbers of multiple killings in the city. After all, this was where David Berkowitz, the Son of Sam serial killer, had just a few years earlier been sentenced to six life terms, or 365 years.

There were, however, several excellent initiatives in the city. One was the Crimestoppers programme, allowing the public to report crimes, identify suspects and provide intelligence tips anonymously. Although the scheme enabled the public to claim rewards, again anonymously using a series of codes, experience showed that New Yorkers were rarely interested in the cash. There were an incredible number of calls about all sorts of crimes including homicides, bank robberies and rapes. When I watched the scheme operating from a small office high up in Police Plaza in Lower Manhattan I knew that there were parts of it that could work well in Scotland.

Equally, a Career Criminal Program operated to ensure that when repeat offenders were linked to a crime, no matter how minor, extra police staff were attached to the investigation to ensure all available evidence was collated to make a conviction more likely. Known criminals caught for minor thefts, assaults and similar offences knew that, given their status as career criminals within the system, the authorities would work hard to achieve a conviction. It seemed to me to be an excellent crime prevention measure in the raw, placing pressure on criminals to avoid committing crime gratuitously. Too often in Scotland 'career' criminals have no previous convictions, however minor, when they appear in court on a serious charge. This happens because witnesses don't want to be involved in prosecuting organised crime figures while, at the same time, police officers accept that minor crime convictions are seldom seen as significant. The New York programme ensured that career criminals felt the full pressure of law enforcement upon them. They knew that, if they stepped out of line, the police would use all their powers to convict them. Again, this looked like a good idea that could work back home.

Another scheme, then in its infancy, was the use of statistical analysis to identify crime trends and patterns in the boroughs. This initiative was the first phase of the performance management system for New York – a management philosophy made famous later by Police Commissioner Bill Bratton and Mayor Rudy Giuliani, the head of City Hall from 1994 till after the 9/11 tragedy. Mayor Giuliani is widely acknowledged as the originator of the Zero Tolerance policing philosophy introduced to New York at this time. The era of 'comstat', when police commanders were grilled about crime and incidents affecting their areas and their perceived successes or failures, was just beginning.

The pressure was being felt throughout the police force although I could not see that it was bringing about results on the streets. To me, New York police officers seemed to have their backs against the wall all of the time. There were far too few officers and, rocked by a series of corruption scandals, the force lacked the confidence that it could succeed.

Patrol officers were not even allowed to accept a free cup of coffee whilst on duty and seemed to feel that they were under continual surveillance from the professional standards units. Given a situation where the same officers ran private companies and took on contracts, these were very difficult contradictions to balance out.

Above all, the one thing it confirmed to me was the universality of police work. New York operated a crime reporting system similar to ours, their headquarters ran a control room and attached operations support just like back in Glasgow and we even laughed at the same jokes.

On or off duty, the officers could not do enough to help me. On one occasion, I was asked to speak about policing in Scotland to a patrol officers' union meeting in Manhattan. I turned up, expecting a couple of dozen people in the backroom of some precinct but I faced a hall with about 400 patrol officers keen to hear about policing in Scotland. They were fascinated to know how we policed without guns. When I showed them my detective's stave, they could not believe police officers could patrol with such primitive equipment. How times have changed!

By August, it was time for me to move on after two months in the sweltering New York heat. Despite many of the shortcomings I had witnessed, I had learned a great deal about the NYPD's response to serious organised crime. Their use of analysts to appraise and report on crime patterns was impressive and I was confident this technique would become significant for the future.

The value of informants would also, I felt, become increasingly important. It was apparent to me that the NYPD had, at this time, lost contact with organised crime due to the impact of corruption scandals in the previous decade. It forcefully reminded me of the ways in which organised crime could undermine the authorities.

After my stint in New York, I had been offered the opportunity to go to Washington to see the US Senate Commission on corruption and then visit Quantico to meet with Federal Bureau of Investigation colleagues. These were small opportunities that don't come very often and I was very keen to take them up.

My arrival in Washington was in complete contrast to my first weekend in New York. NYPD officers had been in touch with staff at the Senate and arranged for me to be met at the airport and looked after. I was met by a former NYPD detective, who had decided that I should stay at his home. However, on my arrival at the airport he told me that his daughter had been seriously injured in an American state many miles from Washington DC. I told him to drop me at a hotel but he insisted I would still stay at his home as he and his wife jetted off to see their injured daughter.

By 5 o'clock that evening I was alone in a beautiful house with a car at my disposal. Relatives called throughout the weekend to look after me. This was the warmest welcome a stranger could hope to receive and I have never forgotten it when dealing with visitors to Scotland. I was treated like a lord throughout my stay and by the middle of the week my host and his wife had returned home as, thankfully, their daughter was now on the mend.

My visit to the Senate reinforced my views about the very real threat the authorities face from corruption initiated by organised crime, and in America's case big business as well. I was very impressed at the open access I had to the American political system and its administration – their commitment to make a difference was evident.

I received an equally warm welcome from the FBI at Quantico. Here I visited the Behavioural Science Unit, where the psychological profilers worked. I was fascinated by their cutting-edge work and the possible areas where the skills they had developed could be applied. In 1985, the unit had recorded significant success helping police to identify several murder suspects accurately. Again, their openness and enthusiasm was extremely impressive.

I also attended the FBI course for agents dealing with paedophiles, which gave me my first insight into the nature of paedophiles and the problems they pose.

I had enjoyed a fantastic summer working with police colleagues in the United States and all my experiences were brought back to Scotland and would influence my thinking in fighting crime. I have been very pleased to see Crimestoppers develop so successfully here in Scotland but I still think that there are plenty more benefits in the Career Criminal Program that could well repay investment.

28
Off to Airdrie –
Football, Casuals and European
Nights

By 1989, I had served as a Chief Inspector at Saracen police office and also spent time seconded to Strathclyde Regional Council. It was a surprise, therefore, when I was transferred again, this time to Airdrie, a market town in Lanarkshire.

When I arrived in Airdrie, the area was under a national spotlight because of a political focus on Monklands Council, which was continually described as inefficient and even alleged by some politicians to be corrupt. One local politician even welcomed me to my new job saying: 'You must have fallen out with somebody to have been transferred here!' It wasn't the greeting I had hoped for but my experience at Airdrie proved that you should never judge a book by its cover. My time as Airdrie police chief proved to be amongst the most satisfying and happiest of my service. Far from being a problem, the council proved to be supportive and open to new ideas, the local community was proud and welcoming and the business community keen to achieve more – if occasionally critical of the police. Even the local football team, Airdrieonians, was tough and hungry for success.

My old-fashioned office in Airdrie could easily have

formed a backdrop for *Dixon of Dock Green* but most of the officers were hard-working and enthusiastic. The area was blighted by the familiar problems – youths with nothing to do in the evening, alcohol abuse and violence. The full impact of drugs was only just beginning to reveal itself in the area. The subdivision covered a large area and my officers spent most of their time driving around it responding to the calls. There were few opportunities for proactive policing. As Chief Inspector, I had five inspectors working for me. My nearest senior officer was based in Coatbridge, about seven miles away, but he might as well have been on a different continent as far as Airdrie was concerned. It still felt like an old market town, with people from the nearby villages heading to Airdrie to shop or go out for the night.

Amongst my duties was the policing of football matches and for almost five years I covered every home game at Broomfield stadium. I had never been a football supporter and the romance of 'the beautiful game' has passed me by, so my first visit to Broomfield was something of a culture shock. The stadium, if that's not too grand a description for Broomfield, was a simple football pitch built, unusually, on a slope and surrounded by a series of wobbly brick walls. On the west side there were changing rooms for the teams and officials. On my first visit I met Alex MacDonald, the manager, who had previously been a player at Glasgow Rangers. He told me that nothing in Glasgow would have prepared me for policing Broomfield – and time was to prove him right.

Although the crowds ranged from 2,000 to nearly 15,000, depending on the opposition, the home supporters were always passionate. The regulars, men and boys, were spread around the ground at their favourite spots and were always quick to give their view on the team's performance, usually with a great deal of humour. Still finding my bearings during the first match, it was clear the manager had yet to win over the Airdrie supporters.

Sitting on benches directly in front of the south stand, Alex received constant abuse from his own supporters. Loudly and continuously, these allegedly respectable supporters questioned his parentage, his sanity and even his honesty. With fewer than 5,000 at Broomfield that day, every shout emanating from the wooden stand resonated around it and blasted into the ground. It seemed unbelievable to me that grown men, frequently with their young sons beside them, could work themselves into such a frenzy. Despite such a warm welcome from the fans, Broomfield was usually freezing cold as it delighted in being the highest football ground above sea level in the country.

By the end of my first match I was starting to acclimatise to the atmosphere. In the final few minutes, when Airdrie pushed forward and won a corner, the home support erupted. The score was still nothing each and this could well be the final chance for the home team to win the game. I watched as an Airdrie player ran up to take the corner kick close to where I was standing. The player looked over to his manager for advice and I sensed Alex was going to say something significant. Alex stood up and pointed behind him to the biggest buffoon in the stand and shouted loudly: 'Ask that bastard what to do. He's been screaming advice all day!' Airdrie was to turn out to be that kind of town. The embarrassed buffoon blushed bright red, became the centre of fans' ribbing, and, for the first time that day, was silenced. The game finished without a goal but everyone had enjoyed their entertainment as they set off home.

Soon, however, my days out at the football were preoccupied with a sinister fringe element that seemed to be set on violence. They were not interested in the football but rather the chance it gave them to fight. These casuals were a strange mix – there were a number of professional people but also ordinary working men and the unemployed. Their status in the gang was decided by their reputation rather than their affluence. In Airdrie, the casuals called themselves Section B. Although I had heard about such gangs, this was the first time I'd experienced what these people were like and how far they'd go to get involved in a fight. For me the match day began five hours before kick-off as I and my small group of officers would plan to spoil the thugs' day out.

It became increasingly obvious that these casuals were also spending considerable time planning their strategy to overcome our defences. Every home game became like a game of chess, with the casuals preparing traps for the visiting supporters while we deployed uniformed and plainclothes officers to prevent the violence. What made them so difficult for us to police was that, if the casuals could not track down their pre-identified opposition, they would turn on innocent law-abiding supporters or sometimes even passers-by.

The casuals would also change their options if they were outwitted. Sometimes they would plan ambushes at the railway or bus station, other times they would lie in wait near one of the car parks, looking to assault the away supporters and damage their cars. In desperation for a fight, the casuals were even known to resort to starting trouble amongst the crowds on the roads leading up to the stadium.

For games against Celtic or Rangers we could count on extra support from police colleagues as mounted units, the police helicopter and additional officers were drafted in. The away supporters on these occasions were largely well behaved, overwhelming in their number, and well organised to return to Glasgow as soon as possible after the match.

For most other matches, though, it was left up to my local officers, with support from neighbouring subdivisions, to police the games. At the time, it wasn't acknowledged that teams outside the Old Firm also had casuals, like Airdrie's Section B, who brought violence and mayhem to the town on match days. With so few officers it was a real challenge to police these games and it was only made possible by the knowledge and expertise of local police officers such as Davie MacIver, who was born and bred in Airdrie. Their knowledge proved to be invaluable on many occasions when the action of a single officer prevented serious violence when the casuals had managed to outmanoeuvre us.

Policing Airdieonians football matches became a way of life for me. I spent every second Saturday and sometimes a week night at Broomfield. When Airdrie made it to Europe, there was a completely different atmosphere as the whole town got behind the team. It was like a carnival in the town as the big night approached with Airdrie taking on the mighty Czech team Sparta Prague.

The day had been long in the planning and, with all my officers deployed to cover the big game, I was standing outside Broomfield when the Czech team arrived. The largest luxury coach I had ever seen was waved through by the pointsmen, as was carefully arranged, and pulled up outside the ground. The powered door slid open and an immaculately dressed, suntanned man, looking like a Greek god, stepped off the bus. He was followed slowly by a group of similarly styled young men. He pushed at the red gate to enter but was surprised to find it locked. The groundsman appeared and asked this stranger who he was. I couldn't hear what he said but was amazed to watch as he had the door shut in his face. I heard later that the groundsman told him that only when he had checked with George Peat, the club secretary that it was OK, would he be allowed into the stadium. What a welcome for our distinguished foreign visitors! A few minutes later the gate was opened finally and the Czech team was allowed into the hallowed Broomfield stadium. The game itself passed off without mishap. Airdrie played well but that Scottish lack of confidence kicked in as the young players took fright and went down 1-0 and their European dreams were soon over.

29
Caught on Camera – How Airdrie Led the CCTV Revolution

Policing Airdrie was always interesting but during 1991 local companies and shopkeepers were becoming impatient because of the high level of vandalism and the large number of break-ins which were affecting their business. Like many areas at the time, Airdrie went through a huge amount of plate glass to replace the hundreds of vandalised windows.

It was clear from the beat officers that a group of teenagers was using a local youth club as a base to carry out attacks across the town. My local officers knew the routine but were seldom able to catch the culprits. They were greeted with hostility by young criminals when they visited the youth club to investigate and the other youngsters present were too frightened to speak out. The management of the club at the time were no better. They were weak and unhelpful but saw the club as a good thing because it gave teenagers somewhere to go at night.

With relationships between the youth club members and beat police becoming fraught, I decided to pay a visit in an attempt to talk through the problem. As you can imagine, I wasn't a welcome visitor. After a robust exchange of views with the young troublemakers, I warned them I would have their club closed if we could not resolve the problems. I prepared to leave. It was a cold, wet Thursday night and it had been a long day. The lack of progress that evening left me depressed as I set off home for yet another 10 o'clock meal. It all seemed such a waste of time.

As I made for the door, a young local girl stopped to speak to me about the meeting. She suggested that the police should put up a camera facing the only entrance to the youth club and monitor it from the local police station. We would be able to watch the comings and goings and match them with the times of the break-ins. It seemed a very simple and effective idea and reminded me of the cameras I had seen in the casinos earlier in my career.

As I drove home for my supper, all sorts of ideas were going through my mind. By the time I was home, I was already really excited by the prospect of placing not just one camera but a series of cameras around Airdrie. Such a system would deal with the problems at the youth club but also help in clamping down on the Section B casuals as well as dealing with the day-to-day criminality affecting the town. Sometimes it's amazing where such ideas come from and how far they can lead.

The next morning I could hardly wait to share my idea with the troops. They were well used to me turning up and changing their long-established routines but this was different. As I explained my plans to the inspectors, I could see the look of doubt in their eyes. I wanted to put up cameras all over the town as well as at the local hospital, which was a couple of miles away. I also planned to monitor the cameras from a base in Airdrie police station and we had designated some office space near the reception area and next to what police officers call the public bar. Despite their scepticism, none of the officers could put up any argument as to why we shouldn't go ahead, though I had no idea how the scheme could be paid for.

First of all, I tried to find out if there were any such schemes anywhere else. It may seem strange now, but back in 1991 there were just two primitive CCTV schemes I could find details about. The first was put in place by a roads engineer in Bournemouth who was using cameras to try and stop street furniture on the seafront from being vandalised; the other was another local authority scheme proposed in King's Lynn, which was designed to provide safe car parks. I thought it would be best if I went to see these schemes at first hand but Strathclyde police headquarters had other ideas and my request to travel to Bournemouth and King's Lynn was refused. I was told that they could see no benefit coming from such a trip.

So, there was nothing else for it. With my wife and daughter, who both knew I would never give up when I had the bit between my teeth, I headed south for a family weekend visit to Bournemouth and King's Lynn. This trip highlighted one key weakness for me in both these schemes – they needed a bigger commitment from the police. Both relied on the police being willing to respond to pleas for assistance from the local authority. However, if police employees could be put in charge of monitoring the cameras, I felt sure a more efficient service could be provided.

I had a clear vision of what I wanted to do but I was only too aware there were many hurdles to overcome and one of the biggest would be issues surrounding people's human rights and civil liberties. I was very fortunate that the local MP was the late John Smith, then the shadow Chancellor of the Exchequer and also a distinguished defence advocate. I met him at the arts centre near the police office and over a cup of coffee we discussed the implications of my CCTV plans. He had a real understanding of the legal issues the scheme would raise but, after some debate, accepted that the benefit it could bring to public safety, crime detection and improving Airdrie's environment outweighed the challenges. He went further and said he would speak up in support of the scheme, if it got off the ground. He also said he would be happy to launch the scheme if I wanted. Having the backing of such a key national figure gave a massive boost to my proposals because it helped garner support from local and regional politicians. It soon enjoyed the political support I needed although getting financial backing took a lot more effort.

Next I brought together an alliance of business interests to form the Airdrie CCTV Development Trust and we met regularly at 7.30am in my office. While the community and business groups worked hard to win support and raise funds, the public-sector bodies began a series of self-analysis and so-called business creation reports. It was clear that the administrative machine was going into reverse and was unable to deal quickly with the needs of a challenging initiative.

The CCTV professionals had advised us that we would need to dig about twenty miles of trenches to connect the cameras up to the police office. On top of this huge expense, we also needed to raise £150,000 to buy cameras, cabling, monitors and other equipment. However, the local support could not have been better. Airdrie was not a prosperous place but, encouraged by local police officers, the community began to raise surprisingly large sums of money. At the same time, the support of the local newspaper, the *Airdrie Advertiser*, was crucial.

By the beginning of 1992, I was confident we could have the scheme up and running that year. I decided it was time to seek the wider support of the general public. The reaction was overwhelming. Despite my fears, there were very few objections. There was a clamour to provide CCTV coverage around the town to improve public safety. Moreover there was a huge amount of local pride at stake as locals sought to ensure Airdrie would be the first town in the country with such a scheme.

In February, I laid out my ambitious plans for that year in a written report to police headquarters and sought permission to go ahead with the necessary building work at the office. I took the absence of a negative reply to mean 'yes' and carried on. The pace of the programme began to speed up and I became concerned about the large number of trenches that were needed.

The cable company NTL had agreed locally that we could piggyback on work they were carrying out between Airdrie and the hospital but the town centre trenches were still a major headache. I went to see Gordon Love, the council roads engineer, and explained my problem. Gordon was no pushover and was well known for his adherence to strict council regulations but he understood clearly the huge benefits the scheme could bring. Later that week, he phoned me to say that he would make sure the roads were dug up during the coming months, as long as I had the workers standing ready to lay the cable and covers. I agreed.

Along with Ian Doole and Margaret McKay, two young police officers working in Airdrie, I began to negotiate with private contractors to get the specialist support and additional finance we needed. By June 1992, there was no going back. Throughout Airdrie the work was frenetic. Back at the police station, the office was being prepared for the arrival of the monitors.

I had approached Remploy, the largest employer of disabled people in the UK at that time, to see if it could provide the staff to monitor the screens in the police office. Remploy was very keen to support me and provided a number of excellent people, largely paid for via a national government grant.

By this time I had promised the people of Airdrie that the scheme would be up and working during the new football season. It was a tight timetable but I knew it was possible and, in October 1992, the system went live. A large number of police officers and friends from the Development Trust watched as the switch was thrown and the first pictures came on to the twelve screens in the new suite specially built within the police office. Local officers watched how eleven cameras covering the main parts of the town were capable of panning, tilting and zooming in to live incidents. The pictures were also recorded on tape so they could be used in the courts. I had negotiated an agreement with the local Procurator Fiscal and Sheriff Principal of the area and we would have had to wait and see if it was worth all the effort.

To allay public concerns about the cameras or about local policing generally, I decided to have a formal launch of the scheme. I invited John Smith MP, now the Labour Party leader, to switch on the cameras at the launch of yet another Open Day at the police office. Once again I sent a report to police headquarters explaining that our CCTV scheme was to be launched by the local Member of Parliament on 7 November 1992. Yet again the invitation was met by silence. As before, I presumed this meant I had been given the green light for the Open Day.

At 7am on that morning I, with all my senior management team, was preparing for the 10am launch when I was called to the phone. I was told the Chief Constable was on the line. Naturally I thought it was a wind-up, but Leslie Sharp was indeed on the other end of the line. He told me that he had had no prior knowledge of my launch but had heard about it on the early BBC news. He just wanted me to know that he would be along later after a Neighbourhood Watch meeting.

At 10am, John Smith was at the police office enthusing about the cameras on a beautiful winter's morning. It was sunny and, although cold, we had a huge public turn out. By the end of the day, 11,000 people had trooped through the police office to view the CCTV system. It was a carnival day and a great success for all those who had played their part in creating the scheme. Everyone came along to celebrate, including local businessmen, shopkeepers, Airdrieonians Football Club, community groups and the many police officers who had painted, sawed and helped in any way they could, frequently working in their own time and at their own expense.

It also became clear that the silence from the administration at Strathclyde Police headquarters was so deafening because someone had thought we would never be able to deliver our CCTV scheme – how wrong we proved them.

A couple of years later, Airdrie hosted the Royal National Mod festival. While I was showing our Highland visitors around the town, an elderly lady from the Islands stopped me in the main street and asked me what Airdrie was famous for. I trotted out my usual responses – the football team, the planetarium and the Airdrie Savings Bank. At the end of her week, this same ninety-two-year-old woman met me again and said that she found out that Airdrie was also famous for its taxis but most of all for its new fantastic CCTV cameras!

30
Diplomacy and Promotion

After five years in Airdrie, it was time to move on, initially to Hamilton as a Superintendent and later to headquarters as Deputy Head of Operations. The headquarters post included the responsibility for overseeing many of the major public order events, including heads of state visits, football matches, parades and the likes.

During my time, I was fortunate to be in charge of a French Presidential visit to Glasgow when President Chirac came with Prince Charles to see Easterhouse. Such events take massive planning, with officers from almost every department deployed in preparing everything from security and traffic management to crowd control and VIP protection.

President Chirac was to visit on 16 May 1996. By the beginning of that month, the whole day's plan, of how we would control the day, was agreed. The Head of Operations always took pole position in the entourage, to make sure everything was running smoothly and make any sudden 'hot' decisions when something cropped up. On such days, it was a pleasure and a privilege to have the best seat in the house and to follow the day's events listening in to the police radio transmissions.

Usually on such occasions, the entourage was preceded by motorcycle outriders from Strathclyde Police. I only once ever saw one of these bikers come off their machine. It was when we were escorting Princess Anne across Glasgow city centre, via Tradeston, having being diverted there because of a motorway accident. It was a typical dark, dank winter's night as we cut through a side street, accompanied by the bikers, who leapfrogged ahead to wave us through the junctions. As one of the bikers passed the royal car on the nearside, he clipped a raised part of the kerb. In the quiet backstreet, it sounded like an explosion and as I reacted to the apparent danger, I saw the strange sight of the biker tumbling and rolling past the entourage in front of his motorbike, which was by now skidding along the street on its side. Having been told in a radio message what had happened, we were able to continue on our way. Fortunately, the motorcyclist was uninjured except for his pride but, needless to say, it was months before he lived it down.

Thankfully the French Presidential cavalcade made its way across the city without a similar mishap. It was a joy to watch the motorcycle outriders speeding along and on this day there were two sets of escorts. As the Prince of Wales and the French President set off for Easterhouse, the Princess of Wales and the President's wife visited the Queen Mother's Hospital.

A week before the President's visit, a delegation of four French security officers turned up apparently unannounced at Strathclyde Police headquarters. As we didn't know they were coming, there was no one except me to meet them. They wanted to discuss security arrangements but it soon came apparent that they expected to accompany the President throughout his visit and be part of the security detail. They were unhappy when I explained that security was solely a matter for Strathclyde Police and their presence was neither required nor helpful.

As the discussion became tense, I feared we were heading for a diplomatic incident but I stood firm. Security was entirely a matter for the Chief Constable of Strathclyde and

I reassured them they could be confident of the force's ability to carry out these duties. However, I promised to provide transport to each venue, so they could keep in touch with all the events. Somewhat reluctantly, they agreed.

On the day, everything ran like clockwork. As the planes touched down at Glasgow Airport on a lovely sunny day, I took my seat, next to the duty Assistant Chief Constable, at the head of the entourage. I saw my French security colleagues step off the plane and then join the back of the delegation.

At the first stop, the President and the Prince went for a walkabout among the crowds in Easterhouse. Obviously, their closeness to the public caused some concern but they received a warm welcome. My French security friends were tense and slightly unhappy at being kept at a distance but they stayed back and did not interfere in any of the arrangements.

At the next stop, it was clear President Chirac was enjoying himself and was keen to get even closer to the public. I could see the French protection officers monitoring our operation from a distance and they quite evidently began to relax – I could see them in the distance smoking their Gitanes.

By teatime, everyone was enjoying the day, which had passed off without incident. I was extremely proud of the entire force as the two groups merged seamlessly together on the M8 at 5pm and headed back to the airport. It was amazing to watch as it all came together at the height of the rush hour. On the airport tarmac, there were at least a dozen cars with various VIPs to see off our distinguished visitors.

I was just beginning to relax and waiting for the plane to take off when my French 'friend' called me over to the door of the plane. As I went up, he surprised me by giving me a Presidential plate to commemorate the visit and he apologised for the upset he had caused at our previous meeting. He also wanted to congratulate the force on the way the day had been handled so successfully.

Of course, not all visits were by such important people but they could be just as significant to the city. The following year, I was summoned one day to the Chief Constable's office to be told I was going Calgary to monitor the Rotary International Conference, which was coming to Glasgow the following year.

I set off to Calgary with Assistant Chief Constable Peter Gibson where we spent the next few days meeting local police and conference organisers to assess the challenge for the coming year. There was also a delegation from the City Chambers led by Lord Provost Pat Lally. On the last night, the Provost turned up in his full regalia to invite the Rotarians to Glasgow. Never one to miss a trick, Pat, after addressing the thousands of delegates, invited a Japanese lady to the podium, having discovered it was her seventieth birthday. The Lord Provost then led the singing of happy birthday and the Rotarians loved it. Ever the professional, as soon as the song was finished, he promised them all the same heartfelt welcome in Glasgow the next year.

The 23,000 Rotarians who came could not all be accommodated in Glasgow and some of them stayed in hotels as far away as Dundee, Edinburgh and the Borders. It was a mammoth task to make sure all these delegates were delivered safely to the Scottish Exhibition Centre in the heart of Glasgow by 10am every day.

Although based at the SECC, the conference used a variety of locations across the city, including Ibrox football stadium. Throughout the week, not one crime was reported by any of the 23,000 visitors. In fact, they enjoyed good weather and a very warm welcome.

One afternoon, a Rotarian dropped a large wad of cash as he walked across the SECC car park. Unknown to him, a police officer, looking out from a high-rise hotel window, had seen him. The officer ran down to recover the cash and searched the centre until he found the man. The visitor couldn't believe the officer's honesty and tenacity – it was clear he would not have expected such service in his home country.

Another evening, a family who were lost stopped a hackney taxi driver for directions. They were ten miles from where they were going but the driver didn't hesitate – he insisted on delivering them himself and refused point blank to take any payment for getting them to their destination.

At that time, my boss was Chief Superintendent John Dale, who was Head of Operations. John had a lifetime of experience in uniform duties and was a very demanding mentor for me. I will always be grateful for his support and encouragement. It was he who pushed me into applying for the Strategic Command Course, the premier training course for officers seeking Chief Officer posts across the UK. One morning, he took me aside and suggested I apply. I was unsure if I wanted to go through this so late in my service but John pointed out that I would end up spending my final years working for less experienced officers. He also promised to phone me at regular intervals from his retirement to remind me of this.

Somewhat reluctantly, I applied and a year later was in an Eastbourne hotel for the two and a half days of psychometric testing, interviews and examinations that made up the Extended Interview. It was necessary to pass the extended interview process before being selected for the Strategic Command Course.

My lingering memory of the Extended Interview was the final day, when I needed to leave by 4.45pm otherwise I would miss my flight home and need to stay another night, which I was not keen to do. I vividly recall going into the final interview at 4pm in hotel bedroom number 242. When I knocked on the door, I was greeted by the strange sight of a man seated at a coffee table with his back to a large window overlooking the seafront. Next to him, there was a large empty space where the bed had been removed, although the headboard was still screwed to the wall. The man, a psychologist, asked me how I felt about the interview and I replied: 'I've never spent an afternoon alone with a strange man in a hotel bedroom before but there's always a first time for everything.'

After I explained my need to catch the plane, I enjoyed a very interesting conversation full of moral questions and political quandaries. As the only successful candidate from Scotland, I soon began the six-month-long Strategic Command Course.

After twenty-seven-years' service, I was appointed as an Assistant Chief Constable in charge of community safety. The move up from Chief Superintendent was to be the most challenging I had made. It took over my life – there didn't seem a minute throughout the week or weekends I could call my own. If I wasn't at meetings, I was on call for firearms incidents or dealing with staff issues. Soon three particular issues were to dominate my life: how police deal with domestic abuse, our response to the Chhokar murder investigation and drugs education.

31
Making the Right
Choices for Life

When I was appointed as the Assistant Chief Constable for Community Safety in Strathclyde Police, I had the chance to really change the way police worked with the community. After a lifetime spent in the police, I know there are three key issues that always concern people – youngsters hanging around, vandalism and dogs fouling the streets. If local police can tackle these issues then that's usually a good start towards addressing basic concerns.

In reality, though, people have a much greater expectation about what they want their local forces to deal with: managing sex offenders; violent criminals; domestic abuse; and the effect of drink and drugs on youngsters. I knew it would be impossible to tackle all these issues effectively, so I decided to concentrate my resources on improving three areas: domestic abuse, drugs education and drugs strategy.

Throughout my service I had always felt that families suffering from violent and abusive attacks received very little help or support at the moment they needed it most. Too often, women were encouraged to take their children away to somewhere safe while their partner was calmed down. On other occasions, family members were left alone while the aggressor was sent out to cool down. Even when there was an arrest, the attacker was taken, usually in a drunken state, to the local police station. There, he would see a lawyer and the Legal Aid process would ensure his interests were protected. Meanwhile, back at home his family was left alone, often in a very distressed state and without any money, fearing what would happen in the days ahead.

In cases where the relationship had broken down irretrievably it was very common for women to be the target of hate campaigns. In the 1990s, police forces were unable to provide any service to these women because there weren't even any IT systems capable of tracking such vulnerable victims. There was also an outdated opinion that accepted one section of society's view that women caught in such terrible circumstances should just put up with it for the sake of their families. The police were unable to provide an effective response and there were similar shortcomings in the other public agencies involved. I knew this had to change.

My new post included being the chair of a subcommittee responsible for domestic abuse issues for the Association of Chief Police Officers for Scotland (ACPOS). The police had already come under pressure from various voluntary organisations, which were extremely quick to point out where police had got things wrong. In fairness, many of these groups were keen to work with the police to help educate and improve our response and effectiveness.

The advice from such women's groups about the pressures faced by women and their families at times of domestic crisis, brought about a significant change in male officers' attitudes. These groups gave the police lectures about the violence, intimidation and fears faced by the families at such times and the difficulties they often faced in giving statements against their breadwinner.

At that time, police officers responding to emergency calls in the middle of the night had no access to information about previous incidents. Many of these cases involved women who had been attacked before or men who were serial offenders against a string of women, but the officer at the scene did not have the intelligence necessary to make an informed decision.

The committee identified the absence of an effective intelligence database to protect vulnerable witnesses as a serious shortcoming. New IT systems were introduced to develop efficient monitoring and this was also driven forward by a Scottish Executive national committee chaired by Lady Smith, who is now a High Court judge, to make sure further improvements were supported by a series of key agencies.

Public sector, private interests and voluntary groups were brought together by our committee to advise the Executive on future measures. Court representatives also acknowledged that judges could play a key role in resolving many of these cases as long as they had the support of the police and social workers, and were given the information they needed.

Compared to the situation twenty years earlier, these changes, as well as the support offered to vulnerable witnesses, improved the response to such cases. This led to a reduction in the number of women facing repeated attacks – attacks which could even lead to murder. There had been cases where the authorities had had knowledge of previous attacks and should have been able to prevent them from escalating to a tragic conclusion.

There has also been a substantial change in attitudes to domestic abuse and violence within our society. Thankfully, people in Scotland are now far less likely to keep quiet or tolerate domestic abuse and there is no doubt this will help us create a better society.

The second area I wanted to concentrate on was the self-evident void in educating our youngsters as they faced the challenges of peer group pressures, bullying, as well as alcohol and drug abuse.

Far too often throughout my police career I saw youngsters who had struggled in primary school completely losing their way at secondary school. At first, they became sullen, disruptive or even violent which could then lead on to truancy and exclusion.

When I spoke to young offenders in prison, virtually every one told a similar tale and that they had lost their way in the first years of secondary school. They started playing truant then followed the lead of others and began drinking, smoking and taking drugs.

Their need to finance a lifestyle of alcohol and drugs led them into the world of crime and to their eventual imprisonment. Many of these youngsters could barely read or write and acknowledged that their lack of basic skills made them virtually unemployable.

I felt there was a need to intervene in the crucial period in a youngster's life to help them understand how they could avoid such pitfalls. If we could support youngsters, particularly during the ages of eleven to fifteen, I believed we could help them avoid a life of crime. We could also help support teachers with better opportunities to educate our children. I knew it would be difficult to find the right message to hold the attention of youngsters at this key age. Any message needed to be clear, concise and delivered in some way that would grab the attention of eleven-year-olds.

One wet Sunday afternoon, I discussed the idea with my wife, who is a teacher, and our then teenage daughter. As we discussed and argued about what might work, the concept of *Choices for Life* was born. I was persuaded that eleven-year-olds were sufficiently streetwise to want first-class entertainment wrapped around a message dealing with bullying, peer group pressure and substance abuse. My daughter insisted that the location was essential – it needed to recognise that the kids could identify it as a place which they thought of as being grown-up and exciting.

After these initial discussions, I had a series of meetings with Barrie Dougall at Strathclyde Police and Alistair Ramsey at Scotland Against Drugs and we formulated the rock concert that now takes place across Scotland every year.

Choices for Life is difficult to comprehend, unless you have been fortunate enough to attend it. The sheer scale is amazing. In 2007, more than 53,000 kids and their teachers attended the concerts at locations all around Scotland, including the Orkneys and the Hebrides.

For most of the youngsters attending the event, it's the first time they have been at a large-scale concert with top quality bands playing. Video clips, quiz shows and finally a drama played out by young people from the Pace Youth Theatre in Paisley all play a part in influencing the attitudes of the youngsters.

Without the year-on-year commitment of staff from across a wide range of police forces and the Scottish Crime and Drug Enforcement Agency, much of that time given without recompense, *Choices for Life* would not take place. People such as Douglas Walker, the head of the Audio and Video Unit at Strathclyde Police, provide the professional experience that is required to bring off a first-class show. Without him and many others, it would have been impossible.

In addition, the children receive 'goodie bags' filled by prisoners from Polmont and Cornton Vale prisons. These contain useful information and souvenirs that the youngsters will use and keep and the bags themselves are often kept for carrying sports gear or as a holiday beach bag.

Since it first began in 1999, the feedback from the schools and youngsters has always been encouraging. What has yet to be found is a way to prepare children with the drugs education they need in the years before the event and, even more importantly, to ensure the continuing message of *Choices for Life* is delivered throughout their time at secondary school. Although I have tried to encourage a holistic approach, I have been unable to persuade the key influencers to take this on board.

I believe that for many years our young people have received confused messages on alcohol and drug abuse – delivered to them at a very vulnerable period of their development. Too many adults prefer to advise youngsters on safety issues, should they decide to experiment with drugs and alcohol. Such a policy fails to recognise that, for many of our children, we are stealing their future and self-respect.

Some youngsters can experiment with alcohol or drugs and come through it but for more than 50,000 people in Scotland, drug abuse destroys their lives. Then there are the many thousands of families and loved ones whose lives it also impacts on.

The harsh realities of these two priorities led me to look at the third area: Scotland's drugs policy – or, as I saw it, the lack of an effective policy. During the next years, I began to develop proposals for a change of approach.

Evidence from academic studies and government statistics showed an ever rising number of registered drug abusers. Though there was an apparent drop in the number of problematic drug users in Scotland during the early 2000s, there was no understanding of how or why this had happened.

At the same time, deaths from drug misuse continued to stubbornly remain at an unacceptable level: around 270-350 each year. As the process of developing a coherent policy concluded during 2006, I discussed the issue with the drugs representatives of all the main political parties. I wanted to try to seek a new cross-party consensus approach to drugs in the lead-up to the 2007 Scottish parliamentary elections.

Top of the agenda of priorities was the need for a clear statement from our politicians that drug abuse in Scotland would not be tolerated. This would be a significant step away from an accepted wisdom that enables services to continue supporting drug abuse by providing harm-reduction advice and support.

In my opinion, the methadone programme, although providing stability for some addicts, had failed to include the key positive aim of returning the patient to a healthy, drug-free lifestyle.

The lack of direction in the methadone programme was clearly demonstrated when officials admitted they did not even know how many patients were taking methadone. There was an air of defeatism in the programme, where some patients had been taking methadone for ten years yet there was no strategy to reduce their numbers or close the programme.

I suggested to our politicians that if we could provide the political vision then the education, health and social workers could then play their part alongside police, courts and prisons services to deliver a reduction in the drug use. The long-term strategy would be to eliminate the increasing numbers of people taking drugs and new recruits to drugs could be reduced through additional work using sport, music, drama and employment to divert our young people to more useful pursuits.

The key to this approach is rejecting the idea that drug misuse is merely a human condition. It is a choice made by individuals who have failed to understand the full impact that drugs are likely to have on their lives.

The United Nations has repeatedly commended Sweden's efforts in showing clearly how positive results can be achieved in such a way. As a country, Sweden is broadly similar to Scotland in many respects. However, it has half as much drug abuse and half our prison population.

I hope that the early indications from our new SNP government of a robust approach to this issue will be supported by the levels of public funding that will be necessary to help us reduce the number of addicts in our country.

32

Seizing Assets and Seeking Justice

In my view, it is essential that the law enforcement agencies and the courts identify, prosecute and convict those engaged in the business of substance abuse, whether they are drug dealers, alcohol and tobacco smugglers or counterfeiters. The seizure of assets from these people is critical to success. When an individual is convicted of being part of the management of an organised crime group, he or she should lose all their assets, whether or not they obtained them from their crimes.

Too often, criminals are able to launder assets successfully through legitimate businesses and into the hands of their friends and family. In such circumstances, draconian powers need to be invoked to act as a deterrent, otherwise law-abiding business people will be drawn into this highly profitable activity. It makes no sense that someone who has handled millions of pounds of drugs pays back thousands of pounds in assets. Whatever other 'businesses' these people own or have control over, they should all be forfeited.

The individuals involved must be identified publicly as the people engaged in the organised crime that is harming our communities. The result of such public identification ensures that law-abiding members of our community, who were previously ignorant of an offender's background, can then distance themselves from these activities to make sure they do not become inveigled into criminality. Equally, the prospect of an effective vilification would act as a deterrent to most sane-thinking people, knowing the impact it would have on their family and friends.

Some of these tactics have been used in other European countries. In Sweden, for instance, a committed approach to reducing drug abuse across the country since the 1980s has seen the levels of substance abuse fall significantly. Sweden is now cited by the United Nations Office on Drugs and Crime as the best example of effective drugs control. There is no reason why Scotland could not follow suit, but it is a long, hard and unglamorous road to achieve such success.

There has been a groundswell of opinion turning away from the habit of illegal drug misuse, according to recent surveys. Complacency has always been the enemy. We all seem too ready to accept the reality of substance abuse in our communities but none of us want to see it in our families.

I have briefed all of the political parties on my views about the menu of options for dealing with substance abuse and, although during my tenure at the SCDEA I would have liked to see more policy movement, I do detect a greater acceptance of some of these views.

In 2007, after my visit to Sweden, politicians and others from the country visited the Scottish Parliament to share their experiences. I hope that our administrators are capable of constructing a new and effective strategy fit for purpose in twenty-first-century Scotland.

In the midst of all this debate about policy and my involvement in the further development of community policing initiatives, came the issues arising from the murder of Surjit Singh Chhokar.

On 4 November 1998, Mr Chhokar was returning home after his day's work as a waiter in a restaurant when he was attacked and murdered for no reason. The investigation into the death led to three men being arrested within six days.

However, the subsequent prosecution of the case in the High Court raised serious concerns about what part Mr Chhokar's race and ethnic background had played. Across Scotland, feelings ran high over the case with many believing that racism had affected the authorities' response to the murder while a minority believed that too much had been made of the case and its outcome.

Three years later, as Assistant Chief Constable for community safety, it fell to me to respond to criticisms of police actions in this case, arising from a report which sought to identify what lessons could be learned from the case. I then had my first opportunity to meet Aamer Anwar, who acted as a spokesperson on behalf of the family. I had already visited Mr Chhokar's family in Lanarkshire and had been impressed by their obvious decency and desire to understand what had gone wrong with the prosecution case.

Mr Anwar was an extremely interesting and challenging young man. As a student at Glasgow University, he had succeeded in a civil action against Strathclyde Police for injuries arising from an assault by a uniformed police officer whilst being arrested.

The success of this case, and his commitment to civil libertarian issues, had led Mr Anwar to become a well-known public figure in Scotland. While most officers would not consider him to be a friend of the police, I could see that his interests and aims were consistent with the objectives set by the force – integrity, fairness and honesty.

Having read the full details of the case, I phoned Mr Anwar to ask him to meet me to discuss his concerns. Initially, I sensed that he suspected my motives but, nonetheless, he agreed to meet me that evening in a coffee shop on Byres Road. I soon realised that here was an articulate and reasonable man. He was clearly someone who would be no pushover for the establishment but, at the same time, he was someone I could understand.

After a number of meetings, it became clear that there were few issues between the police and Mr Anwar, acting as the Chhokar family spokesman. Whilst there had been substantial criticisms of the police, I knew that many of these were based on either misinformation or sometimes just plain mischief.

Throughout my dealings with him, Mr Anwar was pleasant and reasonable, so much so that, after the enquiry, I introduced Mr Anwar to various police groups so that he could explain to them his views on fairness and equality. The feedback from such talks showed they had been worthwhile.

I was also satisfied to read, in Dr Raj Jandoo's report into the Chhokar case, praise for the efficiency and effectiveness of the murder investigation. He stated clearly that he had found no evidence whatsoever of racism on the part of any Strathclyde police officer. As the police force's representative to Dr Jandoo's enquiry, I was satisfied that his report revealed the truth of what happened in this terrible case.

What remains completely unsatisfactory, and saddens me to this day, is that Surjit Singh Chhokar and his family have not received the justice they deserve. We must ensure that this can never be repeated.

33
Trying to Get Out
of Africa

In recent years, I have been fortunate to visit Yaoundé in Cameroon, Tbilisi in Georgia and Hong Kong as well as the United States. Each visit gave me valuable experience and insight into mutual problems and proved beneficial when making decisions back in Scotland. My trips to Africa and Georgia were as part of a delegation supporting Interpol in these areas. Both were challenging in different ways but my experiences in Africa were particularly challenging.

The Air France flight landed at Douala from where it continued on to our final destination of Yaoundé. Once off the plane, I found that my suitcase was missing and all I had to wear were the clothes I was standing in. It was as hot as an oven and, to make matters worse, the humidity was unbelievably high and my malaria tablets were packed in my lost suitcase. Things went from bad to worse as every place in this former French colony refused to take my British credit cards and I had to make ends meet with the handful of dollars I had brought with me.

My hotel seemed to be reasonably well appointed. What put me off, though, were the flying bugs that, to me, appeared to be the size of small helicopters. I have never been good with bugs and they certainly had nothing like these in Partick!

I was also warned it was dangerous to take a dip in the hotel swimming pool because of the waterborne diseases but, given that I only had the clothes I stood up in, the swimming pool was the least of my concerns.

When I checked into my room, I discovered that among the unusual things provided to guests were condoms. Before I could settle, a woman came to introduce herself as someone who could service my needs during my visit. Like the ubiquitous *News of the World* reporter, I made my excuses but the woman was keen for me to realise that there were plenty of other models for me to choose from.

Eating was another challenge. Other than the snacks provided at meetings, every time a meal was served it appeared to be moving about the plate. Any meat served was furry at the edges and I had to survive on just a few boiled potatoes.

After three days, with neither a decent meal nor my own kit in the hot jungle environment, I had had enough. I had been told there was a chance my suitcase could be at the airport. By now I was so desperate that I made my own way there. By a stroke of luck I managed to spot my case in the corner of a store but the guards refused to allow me access to the area. In a fit of pique and probably very unwisely in the circumstances, I forced my way into the room and seized hold of the suitcase, refusing to leave without it. After a few tense minutes, a senior official turned up and after a brisk conversation I was waved on my way. I was very glad to be back at my hotel with my possessions.

I can remember how isolated I felt being on my own in a very difficult situation in a strange country. How much worse it would have been if I did not have the backing of the police service and Interpol behind me.

Thankfully, I was at last able to start taking my malaria pills but the locals told me that gin and tonic was just as effective. Whichever it was, I survived to tell the tale.

There were more problems. Although my plane out had taken me all the way to Yaoundé, the return ticket began at Douala. My office had booked my trip with Air France but there were no Air France flights out of Yaoundé on the Friday – either that or my office did not want me back. Whatever the reason, I needed to book a local flight to Douala but that proved to be extremely difficult. Although the meetings and the company had been good, I was horrified at the prospect of being stuck on my own in Cameroon after everyone else had gone home. Throughout the week, delegates had started heading home and I would be the only one returning via London on the Friday.

The conference centre was more like a rugby scrum than a meeting area. By the Wednesday, I had found my way around the place and had discovered a local woman who would be able to arrange my flight. Fortunately for me, she had previously had links with Scotland and loved my Scottish accent. When I told her about my problem, she said she would personally ensure that I boarded the plane but, for some reason, she did not think I needed a ticket. After some discussion, she agreed to give me a confirmation slip but this was just a scrap of paper with my name written on it. I told her I wasn't impressed. After all, I already knew my own name as I'd had it all my life. What I wanted was a real ticket that would guarantee me a seat. Eventually she relented and arranged to meet me at a city centre office where she said we would be able to get the ticket printed.

The next day I made my way there as arranged. My walk through the city was an education. As the only white face, I soon became the focus of much interest. As I turned yet another corner, I began to feel more and more isolated. There was no rational reason for such feelings as everyone I met had been decent to me all week wherever I had gone. It struck me that I was feeling the same disorientation and strange surroundings that many new migrants to Britain must feel. Of course, the inability to speak the local language just makes matters worse for them, and on this occasion, for me too.

Finally, I found the office I was looking for down a backstreet. The glass-fronted shop had a waiting room and a counter at the reception but, of course, nobody was expecting me. I was shown upstairs and asked to give my details when my friend from the conference arrived to rescue me.

My plane ticket was produced and all I had to pay was £17. It seemed very little for a flight across the country. I was warned, however, that there could be a difficulty with the weather. Heavy rain often caused the Friday flights to be cancelled because of the condition of the runway at Yaoundé.

As I set off in a taxi to the airport on Friday afternoon it was teeming with rain. When I had arrived in the country, I had hardly noticed how basic the airport facilities were. The runway was uneven and was surrounded by heavy vegetation which led into the jungle. The airport was crowded with a vast number of people just there to watch the action.

I managed to push my way to the gate and saw a very small, well-worn plane parked on the runway. It had what looked like a series of patches on the bodywork and appeared it could take just seventeen people.

The heat was stifling and, to make matters worse, thunder and lightning started. Men and women jostled for position at the gate but as I approached, I saw the woman who had sold me the ticket. With her help I soon found myself on the plane complete with suitcase.

We sat on the tarmac for about forty minutes as the temperature rose and the torrential rain kept pouring down. Inside, the plane was as basic as it looked from the outside. The division between the passengers and the two large pilots was a simple patterned curtain hanging half off the rail. There were no stewards on board. Eventually the door closed and we began to taxi across the lake that passed for a runway. The lightning seemed to be following the plane and crashed around us making the passengers nervous and upset. After a bumpy ride along the tarmac, the old plane finally took to the skies heading straight into the storm.

It felt like a scene from the film *Raiders of the Lost Ark* and I sat waiting for one of the engines to burst into flames. Across the aisle, a man sat on a single seat smoking – something I had not seen on a plane for many years.

He had distinct, dark features and a flowing mane of dark hair carefully sculpted to make him look like a film star. When he saw me looking at him, he turned, and speaking in a thick French accent, said: 'You don't appear very frightened by the weather conditions?'

I leaned over to him and replied: 'Given the week I've had, I'd rather die up here than spend another week trying to survive down there.' My new-found friend laughed heartily. He said that life in the Cameroon was a matter of experience and an acquired taste. I knew exactly what he meant!

34
Organised Crime – Capone, the Mafia and Scotland

Most people's earliest knowledge of organised crime harks back to Al Capone and his crew of alcohol smugglers and bootleggers in America back in the 1930s. Alphonse Gabriel Capone was a New York hoodlum who moved to Chicago as a young man to take control of the 'Chicago Outfit'. He sought to create one of the most successful criminal organisations in America. If it hadn't been for Eliot Ness and his 'Untouchables', Capone would never have become known throughout the world but would have just remained a notorious local gangster.

The most interesting thing about Capone was his links to the city council, local and national politicians and his control of the police force. His attempts to present himself as a 'businessman' and his use of corruption have made him a role model for modern criminals seeking to become crime bosses. Although involved in much of the serious crime in Chicago, Capone was never convicted of a straightforward crime. His downfall came after an investigation by Ness into his financial affairs led to him being convicted on tax evasion charges.

Before his conviction, Capone's ability to divert the law

enforcement agencies ensured he could control his criminal empire openly from the penthouse suites of Chicago's most luxurious hotels. If Capone was interested only in profit and money he would not have conducted his business in this way.

It is necessary to understand some of the history of organised crime to comprehend fully what has happened in Scotland during the past fifteen years. Capone's notion of a crime family is drawn largely from the Italian Mafia. The Mafia, or Cosa Nostra, is thought to have been created as a result of the social disintegration of Italian society in the 1848 revolution. Cosa Nostra adopted what appeared to be an honourable persona by suggesting its main purpose was defending the poor and dispossessed. It was soon apparent that the Mafia's real reason for existence was filling its own coffers. Its fiction of a protecting and beneficial role, coupled with corrupt links to police and politicians, protected Mafia members from arrest and conviction and some would say it still does.

Italian citizens understood that the Mafia controlled the authorities and knew that resisting their criminal power was futile. The Mafia, therefore, became part of the establishment and appeared to have a mandate to operate in its own right.

The management of any such crime group today demands the same characteristics of loyalty, secrecy and discipline enforced by a layered series of executives. This arrangement delivers for the organisation a much needed career ladder for gangsters. It also ensures that those earning the most in an organised crime group take the least risk, while conversely those at most risk of arrest or violent attack are paid far less.

A criminal's status relies on his ability to exercise power, influence and control, both within the criminal group and the outside community. The layered structure is, however, not always stable, neither does it always form a simple pyramid. Power, influence and control depend on relationships and knowledge and these can transfer within the group given the expertise of the various criminals and the particular crime involved.

The history of the Triad gang organisations offers similar lessons. Initiated in the eighteenth-century, Triads were originally resistance groups, whose purpose was to overthrow the Manchu Emperor. They used secrecy and discipline and exercised power, influence and control over Chinese communities to try to achieve this objective. Just like the Mafia, Triad members characterised themselves as protecting people from the injustices of the state.

By the twentieth-century, with no emperors left to overthrow, the Triad organisation's original reason for existence had been removed. Its members did not want to lose their position and status but they came under pressure from the strict communist rule. They then regrouped into a criminally focused organisation, whose interests were increasingly based outside China – in Hong Kong and beyond.

Even with my limited personal experience of the Triads, I had learned that Triad members expected the establishment to be corrupt; they expected cash to be stolen or evidence to disappear. Many Chinese businessmen believed that the police would take money from the Triad members and, for this reason, were reluctant to give statements. Triad willingness to use power to force compliance also ensured the authority of the crime groups.

The Triads, just like the Mafia since the 1990s, have developed the muscle to operate nationally and internationally. Many Chinese migrants have relatives in Far Eastern countries where they can be reached by Triad associates and this transnational organisation mirrors the globalisation of legitimate commerce and politics. The Triads emulate such globalisation and are able to operate on any continent, whilst taking account of different geo-political influences.

Britain has developed similar criminal organisations stretching back to the 1950s and 1960s when, for example, the Kray family controlled large areas of London criminality. The Krays, too, conducted the family business in the full glare of newspaper publicity, with close contacts to leading politicians. The twins kept a high profile at charity events and funded boxing contests, attended regularly by highly influential politicians of the time, such as Lord Boothby. If their criminality was merely a means of obtaining access to wealth, there would be no need of such publicity. The need for a high-profile figure continues to dominate today – as can be seen reflected in the recent conviction of the Adams family in London, the Colombian cocaine barons or the new organised criminals now appearing from West Africa. Organised crime figures will always seek to distance themselves from criminality.

These examples clearly demonstrate the essential differences between crime and serious organised crime. Criminals seek cash to provide for their immediate needs but they have no longer-term aims. For those involved in serious organised crime, the provision of a profit just to maintain their living is not enough. They have lifted the 'skirt' of our society and believe that criminals can have significant power, influence and control over their environment. They bring together an organisation that has discipline, management and strategy to create an organised crime enterprise.

Even in Scotland, organised crime figures seek publicity and look to rub shoulders with media personalities, leading sporting figures, politicians and their officials, whether in government or police and law enforcement. In March 2002, Justin McElroy, a convicted drug dealer suspected of being involved in organised crime, attended the Red Rose dinner held at Dalziel Golf and Country Park in Motherwell. The dinner was an annual fundraising event for the Labour Party and senior politicians from the Westminster and Holyrood Parliaments who were present had no idea that such significant criminals were joining them. What was it that made criminals want to attend a fundraiser? In Scotland, organised crime groups act the same way as they do in the United Kingdom and across the rest of the world. They seek to befriend and, thereafter, compromise the legitimate holders of power. In the future, they hope they can use their access, influence and control to benefit their own enterprises. In the meantime, the association with and identification with legitimate authority lends the criminal an air of respectability and power in the minds of ordinary people, who then fear corruption at work in our society. We must be on our guard for such developments in Scotland.

Six days after the Red Rose dinner, Justin McElroy was shot dead outside his home. His murder revealed the close proximity between the legitimate and criminal worlds in Scotland. Had McElroy not been murdered a few days later, many people at the event might still be unaware that organised crime was using the evening to assess what value those attending could bring to their organised crime activities. In the future, all political parties and the authorities face the challenge of denying organised criminals the access they seek.

This same real challenge also applies to officials who provide licensing and planning or authorise contracts for public services. Such opportunities offer criminals the legitimacy they seek, allowing them to launder the profits from their illegal enterprises. Criminals will not pass over any such opportunities. Public and private organisations must be alert to attempts to infiltrate and corrupt their businesses, both internally and externally.

In planning for the future, the police service and law enforcement bodies need to take more account of organised crime. It is self-evident that such criminals will seek to have those who work in the police and law enforcement on their payroll. As investigators have used the advantages gained from the Proceeds of Crime Act legislation and various technical covert aids, criminals have once again turned to attempting to corrupt officials.

This is not new. In 1930s America, the Wickersham Report on Police identified many of the same problems. Today, given official estimates that organised crime enterprise profits across the UK are £18billion, the motivation and capacity to corrupt is all the more pressing.

It is for these reasons that Scotland must have a vibrant and effective Scottish Crime and Drug Enforcement Agency which is capable of researching the activities and intentions of organised crime, so it can then disrupt, arrest, convict and seize the assets of such groups. We have yet to address this issue adequately. It is naive to think that, as long as we have good administration, bureaucratic control and set targets, the Mr Bigs will simply fall into our laps. Such thinking will allow us only to deal with the runners and workers. The top-tier criminal enablers will simply sit back and protect themselves from harm.

The management at the Agency needs a consistent approach which leaves it free to act and to do whatever it takes legally to gather the evidence necessary – without the harassment of efficiency savings, budget cuts and small-time political issues blocking progress.

There is abundant evidence to show that, when organised crime identifies an area where the authorities operate successfully and aggressively, crime groups will move elsewhere to avoid losses and punishment. Over the past decade, as the United States of America administration took a more aggressive approach against the Colombian drug barons supplying cocaine throughout the States, these dealers moved to a new market – Europe. This followed the creation of laws enabling American agencies to extradite drug barons from Colombia to America for trial and imprisonment whilst effectively seizing and freezing their assets.

The drug smugglers did not like the new rules of engagement. It threatened their wealth and undermined their power and influence on the Colombian government. It also ensured they would feel the full rigour of the law, if they came to the attention of the American law enforcement agencies.

In Europe, with our multiplicity of views about substance misuse and liberal approach to transporting goods and people across our state boundaries, we have left ourselves wide open to Colombian drug dealers and smugglers.

Organised crime, whether trading in drugs, counterfeit goods, people smuggling or anything else, knows it will take decades before Europe can prepare itself to deal effectively with the problems they cause. Meanwhile, they can maintain their distance from the business, sometimes even trading from a different continent.

Scotland has the geographical benefit of being off the main track for much of this trade. These groups don't pass through Scotland on their way to trade in other countries so Scotland tends to be the end destination for such networks. It is essential we make our part of this network unmanageable and so costly to organised crime that they will take their business elsewhere in the world.

This should be a key government target for the Scottish Crime and Drug Enforcement Agency. The SCDEA should also be made responsible for gathering together the many strands of intelligence held by various agencies and police forces but not presently collated in the most effective way. Unless one person and organisation is nominated for this responsibility, then there will always be a lack of accountability and effectiveness.

A government taskforce is valuable in keeping the

government in touch and able to remove any blockages. However, committees, panels and taskforces seldom deliver the innovation and commitment of a named individual. After all, that's why we seldom use committees to decide battle strategies in times of war. We nominate leaders and, thereafter, provide the governance and control to ensure effective support. The current arrangement with the Agency being responsible to the Scottish Police Services Authority is not fit for purpose.

35

Drug Wars

My years as Director at the Scottish Drug Enforcement Agency (SDEA) and thereafter as Director General of the Scottish Crime and Drug Enforcement Agency (SCDEA) see-sawed between the most satisfying and the most frustrating period of my police service.

I was fortunate to have been left with a first-class organisation by my predecessor, Jim Orr, but in spite of this, there were continuing reservations from across the policing community about the need for such an agency. Many feared the SDEA would be used to centralise key police services, in a run-up to a single police force for Scotland. Others didn't like the Agency, as it operated within their force area but outwith their control.

When the opportunity came to lead the Agency, in spite of the difficult backdrop, I couldn't get there quickly enough. Jim Orr had been unwell towards the end of 2003, so Chief Constable Willie Rae allowed me to move to my new post almost immediately.

I was fortunate in my newly appointed deputy, Bob Lauder – someone I had worked with for many years and held in enormous respect. I also knew many of the officers attached to the Agency and I knew that, working together, we would be able to give the Agency more impact.

My initial assessment showed that there were two immediate issues for the Agency to take on. The first was to ensure that the Agency had the powers and independence to be able to tackle the Mr Bigs, as the media so often characterises them. It was essential that Scotland should have an equivalent of the American FBI, able to operate freely across police force boundaries and lead the fight against organised crime, unhindered by administrative hurdles. In providing this, the Scottish Parliament had a key role in ensuring that appropriate governance and effective legislation was in place to support the creation of the new Scottish Crime and Drug Enforcement Agency.

The second issue was to maximise the recovery of assets from criminals, while making sure the key criminal targets were those who inflicted the greatest harm on our community.

However, soon after my appointment, a third issue arose when the Home Office reclassified cannabis from Class B to Class C. Although the government advisors thought reclassification would encourage a mature public understanding about the dangers of using cannabis, I believed it would lead to misunderstanding and misinformation. This, in my view, would confuse youngsters and be seen as an invitation to dabble in drugs.

Such confusion also offered an opportunity for criminals who perceived a softening in the approach to cannabis. New markets would open up to take advantage of the young and inexperienced and thereby encourage more drug abuse.

My years at the Agency were divided between advising on policy and strategy on the one hand whilst trying to ensure effective operations were delivered on the other. I wanted an independent SCDEA which would be able to operate under its own authority and with its own staff, supplemented by officers seconded from Scottish police forces. Throughout its history, the SDEA has always suffered a staffing shortfall. There had been a reluctance by most police forces to release key staff to the Agency, as their skills were also needed by their home forces. To overcome the servant and master relationship, I wanted the Director General to have equivalent standing with the exclusive group of Chief Constables who make the key decisions through the Association of Chief Police Officers for Scotland. It is essential to the fight against serious organised crime that there is a strong voice speaking on behalf of the national Agency when decisions affecting funding and policing are made.

Finally, I wanted to see a campus constructed in Central Scotland that would allow all the agencies involved in the investigation of significant crime groups to work together in a more effective way. A Scottish Crime Campus, shared by the SCDEA, HM Revenue and Customs, the Serious Organised Crime Agency, Work and Pensions and the Crown Office, would be the physical embodiment of our nation's clear determination that we would not tolerate Serious Organised Crime in Scotland.

A location more central than the current base in Paisley would encourage more officers and staff from right across the Central Belt to join the fight against serious organised crime. I had even attracted the attention of Lord Foster, one of the world's greatest architects, to the idea. I presented it as an opportunity for him to give something back to the community to repay the good times he had experienced around the world throughout his life. I was grateful to Lord Foster for his enthusiasm for the project. I explained that in time each country would respond to the global criminal threats with a crime campus, allowing all law enforcement agencies across the world to link up internationally. A member of his consultancy team even visited Glasgow to discuss the concept.

Operationally, I readjusted the Agency to target the top-tier criminals, who normally evade law enforcement. The four years I had spent lobbying Scottish MPs for effective Proceeds of Crime legislation had paid off as the new powers were enacted.

Agency staff proved themselves up to the challenge. During my first eighteen months, more than £75million of illicit drugs were seized and significant progress was made to identify the key criminals organising serious crime activities across Scotland.

Our links across Europe were helped by the support of Europol, the key European law enforcement body which helps law enforcement agencies deliver effective investigations. These changes led to our involvement with Dutch, German, Turkish and Iranian nationals, as well as home-bred criminals.

A surprising number of previously unknown criminals came into the frame as a result of our new focus, like Jamie Stevenson and John 'Piddie' Gorman. The sharpening of our intelligence and operational systems revealed strong links between Scottish criminals and Europe.

36
Cannabis – Reclassifying Reason

In 2004, the Home Secretary David Blunkett controversially decided to reclassify cannabis as a Class C drug. For months, there had been media debate about decriminalising, reclassifying or even legalising the drug.

Much of this debate had stemmed from police operational practices in England where officers had been encouraged to ignore possession of small quantities of cannabis to allow them, it was said, to concentrate on other matters. Police commanders, particularly in London, had been encouraging their officers to turn a blind eye to the possession of small amounts of cannabis in public areas.

I fundamentally disagreed with this approach on a number of levels. If Parliament wanted the police service to ignore crimes they could enact legislation to clarify exactly what constituted an offence under the Misuse of Drugs Act. Decisions about what was an acceptable amount of cannabis to possess, the age of the person involved, and issues that could aggravate the possession of the drug are not, in my opinion, best made by police officers on the ground, who are often trying to deal with other public order issues at the same time.

Most importantly, though, I believed strongly that youngsters would be confused by the message that the

217

reclassification of cannabis would deliver – they would believe that cannabis was not considered dangerous.

Whilst the experts thought by reclassifying cannabis they were delivering a subtle message indicating the various levels of danger attached to different drugs, I felt our communities were not sufficiently knowledgeable to respond to that subtlety. I thought that many young people would just misrepresent, or deliberately misunderstand, the message for their own ends.

After reclassification, the police in England and Wales soon found themselves in a dreadful muddle trying to explain in what circumstances discretion was to be used by officers on the street and exactly what quantity of drug reflected personal use.

In Scotland, we have a separate legal system and different policing culture. As the spokesman on drugs issues for the Association of Chief Police Officers for Scotland (ACPOS), I made it clear that, as far as the possession of cannabis was concerned, it was business as usual; all cases involving cannabis possession were to be reported to the Procurator Fiscal.

It was difficult to get our message across. At the time the media were reporting developments in England almost every day as if they reflected the UK position, which patently wasn't true. Prisoners had told me constantly that their problems usually began with alcohol abuse and that this, in turn, led to drug misuse, often starting with cannabis, which then led them into a life of crime.

I also had suspicions that cannabis was not the 'safe' drug many people were so keen to suggest at that time. I explained my frustrations to colleagues in England and Wales and also to the Home Office. I feared that the confusion created around cannabis would present an opportunity for organised crime to move in to what they would see as a soft target – as proved to be the case.

I was determined that we should gather the information to demonstrate the true impact of cannabis on our communities. By February 2006, I felt I had enough evidence to appeal for reconsideration of classification. I was convinced that cannabis was a very dangerous drug causing substantial harm, particularly to young people, and decided that the ACPOS drugs conference for that year should look further at cannabis.

Staff at the Scottish Crime and Drug Enforcement Agency gathered an impressive array of speakers who would outline the dangers of cannabis. Professor Robin Murray, from King's College, London, explained the increase in the number of youngsters being treated for mental health issues as a direct result of abusing cannabis. A drugs researcher showed how the new commercial cultivations of cannabis, which were becoming the norm, were significantly stronger and likely to cause damage to the brain, particularly young male brains which were still developing. In addition, a representative from the United Nations Office on Drugs and Crime brought together evidence from all over the world which pointed to the conclusion that cannabis was indeed a very harmful substance.

Finally, in Scotland we had the recent experience of commercial cannabis cultivations or grows which, in eighteen months, had gone from virtually nothing to sixty-five substantial grows across the country. This reflected the ability of organised crime groups to take advantage of what they saw as a market opportunity, presented by the apparent softening of attitudes to cannabis.

This was not a message everyone wanted to hear and there was an obvious friction over the issue. However, two English Chief Constables who attended the conference headed south calling for a reassessment of the current policy whilst media attitudes began to change. On 18 March 2007, the *Independent on Sunday*, which had long campaigned for the decriminalisation of cannabis, printed a front page apology for this campaign.

Based largely on the same evidence we had presented at our Scottish Conference, the newspaper produced eight pages supporting calls to reassess the UK approach to cannabis. Scottish opinion had led the way on this issue, and rightly so. In May 2008, Home Secretary Jacqui Smith reclassified cannabis as a Class B drug.

Whilst the classifications in the Misuse of Drugs Act might have been useful back in 1971, today I think the different classifications merely confuse. Possession of all narcotics should be acknowledged as illegal. It should be for the courts to decide a suitable sentence, having heard the evidence and considered the harm to the community in each case.

Possession of cannabis in certain circumstances can be just as harmful to a community as supplying heroin. There have been a number of horrific murders and examples of extreme violence by some youngsters who have abused cannabis. The use of the classification of drugs adds nothing to our understanding in such circumstances.

At the same time, it is also essential to confront the current celebrity culture that makes substance abuse appear attractive and exciting. Pete Doherty, Kate Moss, Amy Winehouse and many others over time do immense harm when, by their example, they encourage young people down the road of abuse. Wealth and stardom provide people to help protect them and look after them when they get into trouble. Youngsters living in housing schemes across Britain don't have their advantages. Taking drugs often leaves youngsters ill-educated, sick and lacking prospects. They don't have minders to help them or health farms to treat them – it is a reality we need to confront.

All too often, big businesses overlook the excesses of their stars and invest in the new-found notoriety substance abuse brings to achieve greater profits. In moral terms, how confusing is that for our young men and women? How can we criticise the young and inexperienced when they follow such role models?

If we fail to confront the threat of a rising tide of drug abuse we will find that our public services will be swamped by the demands made on them. Currently, one per cent of the population is involved in substance abuse and the health and social services are already strained and overloaded. If that were to rise to just two per cent, these services, and the justice system, would be overrun without a massive increase in public funding. Can we afford the current policies?

37
Operation Folklore – Jailing Jamie Stevenson and John 'Piddie' Gorman

Escaping from the daily policy frustrations attached to the bureaucracy of the Agency, it was always refreshing to return to the honest world of crime. Among the targets identified by the Agency was a group of men thought to be involved in drug dealing, money laundering and other serious crimes. The four-year Operation Folklore was launched after Agency staff linked James Stevenson and John Gorman with significant crimes that caused considerable harm across Scottish communities.

Had the Agency staff stuck to the traditional performance indicators, Folklore would not even have made the grade. Stevenson had first come to police attention through his links with the McGovern crime family in the north of Glasgow. He was relatively unknown until the murder of Tony McGovern outside the New Morven pub in Springburn in September 2000. Although the McGoverns had been widely identified as a major crime family, their various 'foot-soldiers' were mostly unknown to the public.

After Tony McGovern's murder, it was touted widely around the city that Stevenson had taken over many of the family's interests. Stevenson was questioned and was the subject of a police report to the Procurator Fiscal in relation to the murder. However, subsequently no prosecution followed. At that time nicknamed 'The Bull' by the media, Stevenson quickly became a notable figure in city centre clubs and discos. Criminals acknowledged his significance as a main Scottish player and his name appeared regularly as a key figure in gossip and the print media.

Stevenson had an uncanny knack of disappearing whenever police showed any interest in him. No one seemed to know where he went or what he was up to. These disappearances also upset the crime clans, as they liked to keep tabs on each other. In addition, his absences made it difficult for the Agency to profile him and many people would have decided that he was too difficult to target and picked an easier challenge.

John 'Piddie' Gorman, on the other hand, was a traditional Scottish criminal. He kept a high profile and was quick to show off his affluence and influence. In spite of some of his family being affected badly by drug abuse, Piddie made no secret of his business to the criminal community. He enjoyed a luxury lifestyle built on his life of crime. Even in court, he purported to be a builder but, in months and years of surveillance, the Agency teams never saw Gorman visit a building site or even look as if he had been working at one.

Piddie's wealthy lifestyle was the envy of fellow criminals but it was built on the misery and penury of thousands of Scots. His success made him a role model for many youngsters wanting to emulate his lifestyle, so I was particularly keen to make him an Agency target.

During the first year of our covert investigation into Stevenson and Gorman, we identified their associates. Good intelligence and common sense led Agency officers to trace and stop an HGV lorry on the M74 which contained more than 130 kilos of heroin, as well as a loaded firearm. The driver, a pawn in the wider criminal enterprise, admitted his involvement and was jailed. The recovery led to a flurry of activity, first by Gorman and then Stevenson.

Both men became highly conscious of police tactics and engaged in a series of 'gang meetings' with associates to discuss what the police might be doing.

Those attending the meetings were particularly sensitive about nearby strangers. Gang members even challenged innocent members of the public and searched them for radio equipment and anything else that might identify them as police officers.

We were never discovered but officers did watch with amusement as the criminals went about their security checks. On one occasion, Stevenson, paranoid and concerned about the Agency, believed workmen in his street were police officers. He was so concerned that he arranged checks to confirm the identity of the workers. He never knew that we were watching him trying to watch us, as he was watching them!

During these years, Stevenson became increasingly withdrawn and spent a great deal of time disposing of, transferring or acquiring legitimate assets. Stevenson, along with his stepson Gerard Carbin, was channelling money into a fleet of taxis as well as property development.

By this time, we had electronically bugged a number of places frequented by Stevenson and Agency officers listened to his conversations for months to try to work out his next moves. These tapes, which all had to be transcribed laboriously, would provide evidence for the Procurator Fiscal in any prosecution.

It became clear that Stevenson was trying to clear his decks and prepare for his defence against a prosecution. He even tried to arrange for a psychiatrist to appear as a possible defence witness and sought to engage innocent people, hoping that his story would bamboozle a jury.

Gorman, meantime, behaved very differently and was

impatient for his next drug importation. Watched by teams of investigators, Piddie made some strange contacts, including a previously unconnected man, Douglas Price. Price was a sea captain with a dubious background and by the turn of 2005 he was being kept under constant surveillance by Agency officers.

When Price headed to Europe, the game was on, as it was obvious something was about to go down. At this stage, we didn't know what their game was or even what rules we were playing by. Whatever, the public purse was going to have to pick up the cost.

At this stage, it would have been all too easy to have taken fright but I believed that the Agency should engage with those planning and executing serious organised crime. We needed to clarify Price's true intentions. I authorised Agency officers to travel to mainland Europe. It was a do or die moment and having been in for a penny, we now had to spend many pounds.

Part of me was frustrated at the length of time things were taking. Agency officers were sitting around Europe waiting for the action to start. I knew all our staff felt frustrated but I also knew that the targets had been very successful because they had taken great care to ensure their own security.

At the same time, I was coming under pressure from administrators about the personnel costs and how we purchased services – there was no sense in this at all. Whilst the Minister was happy with what the Agency was doing, the bureaucrats had their own agendas. They were uncomfortable because they did not have direct and detailed control of the Agency. However, if they had that control, the effectiveness of the Agency would be severely tested. They wanted to control the Agency without accountability but there was no way I would allow that to happen.

In spite of such interference, we started to make some progress. With significant support from the Spanish,

Portuguese and Europol, we discovered our captain had taken a new post in charge of a trawler, MV *Squilla*. Captain Price had been busy recruiting an unlikely crew that included Billy Reid from Glasgow as well as an Estonian and a Moroccan.

In the New Year, there was a continual expectation of a 'big turn' about to happen from our unlikely seafarers whilst we had to deal with the ongoing enquiries from the bean-counting bureaucrats.

Weeks passed without any activity. The daily updates sometimes merely reported the crew tanning themselves on deck or having been for a haircut – other days there was even less to report. Price and the crew sat in various ports and sailed off the southern Spanish coast and around Gibraltar. Throughout the operations, we had fantastic co-operation with local law enforcement but, by June 2005, my patience was wearing thin.

Stephen Ward, the operational head of the investigation, was well aware of the pressures faced and the huge costs involved. The intelligence officers knew we were looking for them to give us cause to move in, but it just wasn't happening. There were those outside the Agency happy to give their judgement on our apparent lack of success. Results would come, but we would need to be patient.

In June 2005, MV *Squilla* finally set sail for the Atlantic near to Cadiz. We had had similar sailings before but the captain had been for another haircut and the crew looked set for business. Yet again the Spanish authorities pulled out all the stops. Intelligence linked the group to cocaine and the use of a trawler suggested a large consignment. We were not going to let this one get away.

In the end, we had to rescue the crew. They were so greedy that they overloaded the ship with eight tonnes of cannabis resin with a street value of £24million. We had spent months watching, checking and gathering evidence – but was it enough to prove their guilt?

On 26 April 2006, Gorman was jailed for twelve years after being found guilty at the High Court in Glasgow of supplying heroin, cocaine and cannabis with a street value of £362,000. He was also found guilty of laundering £178,125.

There was huge satisfaction at the Agency at the massive £24million recovery, although some staff would have preferred it if the cargo had been cocaine. Nevertheless, the impact on the Central Belt of Scotland would be significant.

Criminals had spent a fortune funding the boat, the crews and paying their living expenses in Spain for the months leading up to their arrest, as well having to pay for the cannabis resin. Their losses were at least £1million. In addition, many crime groups in Scotland would all have been looking for a pay day from its sale on our streets which would have added to their pain. Due to our disruption and the arrests, the crime groups met to assess the damage and to try to work out if the police had identified their involvement. When criminals spend time worrying about the police, it reduces the time that they can spend on planning future activities – it's a wonder to behold.

While all this was going on, another Agency team was gathering information on Stevenson and his group who, although connected with Gorman, operated separately. Stevenson and his gang met to assess any damage caused by police infiltrating his operations. Unfortunately for him, he could find no evidence of what we were up to, although he knew we were after him. Once again he disappeared but we now knew where was heading as we had traced his Dutch bolthole. We had Stevenson – we merely had to wait for the paperwork and evidence to come together.

Operation Folklore came to a dramatic conclusion in September 2006 when sixty Agency officers supported by a similar number of officers from Strathclyde Police raided fifteen houses and businesses in Glasgow, East Kilbride and

Holland. In the end, nine people were convicted and more than £61million of drugs recovered.

Money laundering charges were proved and assets were being recovered by the Crown. James Stevenson and his stepson, Gerry Carbin, were arrested along with a number of his gang. The media had now nicknamed Stevenson 'The Iceman', allegedly because of his ability to keep his cool under pressure and display his 'bottle'.

As soon as the identity of those arrested became known, the impact was immediately felt by other serious crime groups across Scotland. One prominent criminal told police: 'If you can get to Stevenson, you can get to any of us.' Given Stevenson's reputation at protecting himself from police interest, his conviction sent a massive shockwave across the criminal underworld.

Although non-committal throughout his formal interviews, Stevenson had wilted visibly before interrogators. As chapter after chapter of the evidence was presented to him, he offered no response. At one stage on his way back to the cells, Stevenson turned to a detective officer and muttered: 'I'm fucked here, aren't I?' He was to be proved right.

The High Court was to hear how, throughout the investigation, we had used listening devices to record conversations between Stevenson and his associates. It was evident that, when Stevenson was alone, he was feeling the pressure of our investigations but he could get no feel for what we had on him.

In reality, we had an abundance of evidence proving his involvement in money laundering but we were unable to connect him directly to other crimes involving drugs, due to a lack of solid evidence. Top criminals such as Stevenson are never involved directly with the commodity and this saved him from further charges.

Stevenson had come a long way since being questioned over the murder of Tony McGovern all those years before.

In April 2007, Stevenson and Carbin pled guilty and were convicted at the High Court in Glasgow of various money laundering offences. They, as the prosecution advocate Sean Murphy stated, were 'part of a group which was responsible for laundering substantial sums of money arising from drug trafficking, including the trafficking of Class A drugs.'

In extremely tricky circumstances, the Crown had held together a very complicated case and, against all the odds, had convicted the principal target. James Stevenson, previously thought untouchable and beyond the law, was described as a car valet and jewellery trader. Throughout the years of investigation, Agency staff never once saw Stevenson do one day's honest work. He lived off the backs of decent people and profited from the misery inflicted on Scottish communities, just like the others engaged in serious organised crime.

At the conclusion of the case, Lord Hodge, the trial judge, said Operation Folklore was 'a big success because, all too often, it is the small players who are detected and punished.' An underworld source told the newspapers that the conviction had made it clear to crime groups that they were no longer safe anywhere, not even in their own homes. That is the message I wanted to deliver to each and every member of organised crime families in Scotland.

38
My Father's Death

In 2004, my father confirmed he had a cancer which had first shown its symptoms at our Christmas lunch in 2003. He hadn't seemed himself then and couldn't eat his usual fill of turkey and trimmings. Having retired twelve years earlier, my parents had spent the previous ten years living in a small house with a garden on the outskirts of Glasgow. My father had ended his working life looking after his beloved horses with the Mounted Section of Strathclyde Police.

My father made very few demands on me and I saw him almost every Sunday afternoon when we spent the afternoon talking. At sixty-five, he hadn't been happy to retire as he felt he still had some time to give to his horses. I had realised, however, that he was no longer as strong as he had been and it seemed the right moment for him to take some time for himself. My mother, for her part, while enjoying the peace and tranquillity of retirement and pottering about in the garden, missed living in Partick and seeing all the shops.

I knew my parents could have made so much more of their retirement but I realised, at the time of his cancer diagnosis, that my father was an extraordinarily contented man who wanted for nothing. Although never a gardener, he took satisfaction from the work and the peace and tranquillity he could enjoy in the garden. I had also marvelled at how increasingly close my parents became with each year together during retirement.

Throughout all my adult years, I never heard a rough word from my father. From the moment he confronted his demons and gave up drinking, he never once took a drop. He put his chaotic lifestyle behind him completely.

His one shortcoming had been smoking cigarettes but he even gave that up a couple of years after retiring, realising the dangers to his health. He was honest enough to admit that he enjoyed smoking and missed it. As a lifelong non-smoker, I find it difficult to understand the attraction.

Soon after his diagnosis, it became clear to me that he was not going to survive, so I needed to make plans. Such things have a way of sneaking up on you and I had never thought how I would face up to it. No one wanted to say the inevitable, particularly my father, as he started to decline. By the time it was obvious he was not going to pull through, he was in a terrible state and in agonising pain. He had cancer in his liver, digestive system and right through his body.

The strong, capable man who knew no fear had become like a scared child, wasting away before my eyes. Shakespeare's 'Seven Ages of Man' was ever present in my thoughts as I watched him enter his second childhood and head for the end. I have, as a result of his illness, an immense regard for the Macmillan nurses who treated him during his final weeks. My mother became his constant support and maid, using her nursing skills to best effect. In spite of her age and her own problems, she spent day and night making sure father was as comfortable as possible. Nothing was too much trouble. Their tenderness together was a great comfort to me.

As usual, I was committed heavily at work at this time and was not available as much as I should have been to speak with my father. He was, in any case, very much someone who kept himself to himself and had seldom been a person who talked about his thoughts and reminiscences. He was a practical man who dealt with realities – possibilities and ideas were not for him.

For reasons that weren't apparent at the time, Dad began to see the local Catholic priest in the months leading up to his death. Throughout my childhood, he had rarely been involved with religion and didn't seem to have an interest in the Church. Nevertheless, he wanted to see a priest and to my surprise, the local priest came regularly and they spent time sitting in the garden taking in the sun, with the birds and the wind blowing through the trees. I have no idea what they talked about but I could see my father received great comfort from the young priest's visits, for which I am eternally grateful.

It was only later that I learned that my father had been committed to the Catholic Church but had lost his faith when, as a young man struggling with his alcohol addiction, one Friday night he had knocked on the priest's door at St Peter's Church in Partick only to be sent away, in no uncertain terms, by the priest. I have no doubt that priests must tire of drunks knocking at their doors in such circumstances but my father never forgot this rejection and 'blamed' the Church for abandoning him at his moment of need.

As he waited to go into the hands of his God, he had found the Church again and thankfully also found a priest who lived up to his expectations. I believe that, knowing his death was imminent, my father returned to the Catholic faith he had had in his childhood because he found the prospect of dying without the Church too frightening. Whatever his reasons, there is no doubt he was at peace and his mind serene after speaking with the priest. So much so that he had wanted his body to be held in the Church for his funeral.

For some reason, I suddenly wanted to take my father back to see one of the police horses he had looked after with such love and attention. As fate would have it, that very weekend I read an article in the *Herald* about a Glasgow police horse,

Fergus, who was enjoying his retirement in the Stirlingshire hills.

Ronnie Paterson, my civilian driver at the time, said he would contact the farm and try to arrange to visit Fergus. By this time, my father was in a very sad state; sometimes he seemed only half alive. One minute he could be alert and vivid, the next he was in a semi-comatose state.

Dad was thrilled when I told him that Fergus was still alive and I had arranged a visit; he even seemed to rally. It was a difficult trip to take him out but I was helped by Ronnie, who insisted on driving and helping in any way he could.

My father dressed in his familiar suit and tie, every bit the good and respectable man he had been throughout his life. As he struggled to get into the car, this once strong, muscular man looked shrunken but all the way to the farm he behaved just like a child on a day out. He was just so excited at the prospect of being reunited with an old friend who he was certain would recognise him.

At the farm, we were met by the owner Melanie Reid, who I later discovered was the journalist who had written the article about Fergus. Melanie couldn't have done more. She had even moved an armchair from her home into the barn so father could sit comfortably with Fergus. The horse came out of its stall and instantly recognised an old friend. Fergus's ears pricked up to show his obvious pleasure and my father was more animated and happy than he had been for years. We stayed for an hour and, while Melanie provided tea and biscuits, my father had brought cut apples for his old friend. When it was time to go, I could see my father was tired but content.

Within the week, Dad was dead. It was almost as if he had stayed alive just for that one day 'on the range' and afterwards the power had gone out of him.

Two days after the visit to Fergus, I dropped into my

parents' house on the way back from Edinburgh one evening, something I never usually did. I saw the nurses making him as comfortable as possible for his final hours. When I went into his bedroom, he stirred and said: 'Graeme, I've been waiting to see you, son.' When I replied, he drifted off and that was the last time I spoke to him.

He had been in such terrible pain that the sleep, although probably a coma, was a relief in itself. I left my mother alone with him. They had lived their life together and I felt they should have this time together.

I wasn't surprised when my phone rang at 5am; it usually did for an important work-related call. This morning it was my mother telling me that father had gone. Going back to their house, I was grief-stricken by the sight of him lying dead in his bed but at last he was at peace, his journey over.

Dealing with my father's death made me think about the importance of putting all our time to best use. Making every day count had always been a byword for me but the suddenness of these events made me even more sensitive about the need to get things done.

I think that the experience of my father's death also galvanised my thoughts about my work. Developments, in my view, had just about stalled.

39
Hologram Tam and
into Retirement

While busy on Operation Folklore, the SCDEA staff were also involved in a number of other investigations. Operation Fender was launched after suspicions that a team of forgers were producing top-quality banknotes in Glasgow.

In October 2006, Metropolitan Police officers had reported an unusually high number of fake Bank of Scotland £20 notes being recovered in London. By the New Year, the notes were turning up in banks across Britain. Our English colleagues had contacted the Agency after their trail to Scotland ran cold.

I, and a number of Agency staff, knew there were very few people who had the skill and equipment to produce these notes – Tam McAnea and John McGregor were two of them. Back in 1988, both of these men had been convicted in an earlier plot to flood Europe with fake banknotes. They had also been suspected of forging Old Firm football tickets. However, both had been freed on appeal and had their convictions quashed on a technicality which, ironically, related to a misprinted date on a warrant.

Our surveillance and intelligence operations soon showed that the suspects were working out of a unit in St George's Road, Glasgow, trading under the name Print Link. Weeks of surveillance showed a number of known criminals coming and going from the premises. Soon we had identified seven people connected to the shop. It was a fantastic result and Tam's good fortune was finally about to run out.

When the shop was raided on 28 January 2007, John McGregor had just started a print run of half a million pounds in Scottish banknotes. Simultaneously, other Agency teams searched private houses around the country and recovered a further €406,000. There was also evidence of forged identity cards and drivers' licences. In addition, a large photograph of a High Court Judge adorned the wall of the print room. Beneath the picture of Lord Cameron was scrawled: 'Go on yersel big man' – in praise of the judge who had freed them on their appeal.

Yet again, the officers and staff at the Scottish Crime and Drug Enforcement Agency had delivered a great result. Although there was still the significant job of preparing the evidence for the court, we knew that 'Hologram Tam' (so named because of his rare skill of attaching holograms to make the fake banknotes look more authentic) and his team were, at last, facing justice. There was a mass of evidence from computer programs and banknote paper which would prove their guilt.

On 2 October 2007 at the High Court in Edinburgh before Lord Bracadale, Hologram Tam, John McGregor and five others were sentenced over their counterfeiting activities. The gang received a total of twenty-two years for printing and distributing the fake notes. At the time, it was claimed that the gang had the ability to destabilise the UK economy, had their enterprise not been disrupted.

During my four-year period in charge of the Agency, we recovered more than £125million of illicit drugs, seized firearms, tackled human trafficking and reported millions of pounds of criminal assets for the Crown to pursue.

Unfortunately what I was unable to tackle head-on was the continual interference from civil servants and administrators frustrating the SCDEA's development as a stand-alone agency. Although positive statements were forthcoming, from all and sundry, the reality was a new oversight arrangement for the Agency which was wholly inappropriate. The Agency became a maintained business unit within the group that included IT, police training, forensic science and corporate services and others that made up the Scottish Police Services Authority.

Instead of empowering the SCDEA to deliver on serious organised crime, civil servants pursued their desire to tidy up what they saw as the need for a neat administration. As the election loomed, Scottish politicians were distracted. In that vacuum, the administrators began delivering what they wanted.

Decisions began to be taken without consulting the SCDEA, forcing changes within the Agency which were unhelpful and counter to our strategy. The lack of candour throughout this period was enormously tiresome. I knew, from my appearance at the Justice Committee in the Scottish Parliament and from discussions with various Members of the Scottish Parliament from all parties, that there was cross-party support for a powerful and effective Scottish FBI equivalent.

What was now being constructed was an additional layer of administration within a costly and old-fashioned structure focused on efficiency savings and rationalisations. At the same time, the much-vaunted Crime Campus, which had been announced by the Scottish Executive, was slipping from view. I had first raised the idea of the Crime Campus at the end of 2003 and it received political support early in 2004. Now it was slipping further into the future and I understand that it might not be built before 2012.

The SCDEA and the pressures under which the staff operated meant that the campus was needed as soon as possible, not in the next decade. Much of the work in the Stevenson case was conducted from a store cupboard, which is now being used as an office for four staff; it's never like that on *CSI Las Vegas*.

The Agency needs to be better located to cope with security and protection of both staff and its systems. Some administrators disagreed about the need for a new campus and just wanted a redesign of the current offices. Unfortunately, my link with Lord Foster was not kept up and I felt too embarrassed to report to him annually that the project was still on the horizon.

Given that I had fewer than three years left, I decided reluctantly that, in the ongoing circumstances, it was time to retire and leave others to take on future developments. I also hoped that by stepping away, which for me was immensely difficult, that others would take another look at what was happening and think again. Major mistakes were being made and, in all conscience, I could not be party to those mistakes. My continued presence would be taken as a confirmation of the new strategy – an endorsement.

After the election, Kenny MacAskill, whom I had known as an opposition MSP, was appointed as the new Justice Secretary. I became aware that he wanted me to stay on but I realised that, as he was new to the job, it would take him time to find out what needed to be done.

In fairness, Mr MacAskill took time to speak with me and to try to persuade me to change my mind. I was very grateful to him for his effort but, without an imminent change in policy direction, I had to go. In November 2007, I left the SCDEA for the final time, having being given a rousing send-off by the staff. I felt many ghosts from my past flirting with me as I left the site that day. In my heart, I knew I could not continue with the frustrations of dealing with people at the SPSA and the civil service who would not listen and were determined to distract me from the main task.

Conclusion

In my busy police career so many important events happened and I met so many interesting people that it has been difficult to capture more than a flavour of it here. As a result, this account offers a snapshot of what I was thinking at the time and how I worked during nearly forty years of police service. Nevertheless, I hope that it conveys the sheer thrill and enjoyment of my life in the Scottish police service and will encourage youngsters to follow in my stead.

I have had a fantastic career and the job has made me what I am today. Like any career, it has not all been a bed of roses but, without question, the sense of satisfaction has far outweighed any disappointments. There are those who spend their lives criticising and attacking the police, whatever we do. However, I know that, day in and day out, thousands of police officers across Scotland give of their best in the service of others. Some even pay with their lives. Society needs to remember this and be thankful that there are still people willing to take on such challenges. With that gratitude comes a responsibility.

For the future, our political leaders must find the courage to improve the organisation of the Scottish Police Service and outline clearly the expectations placed upon those in the service. Their current silence on this issue is deafening. There is a need for a clear statement of the way ahead. I believe that the structure of eight police forces in Scotland is unsustainable in the twenty-first century. Created in the 1960s for the 1970s, this structure is no longer fit for purpose.

I also believe that our nation's drugs policy is in dire need of a revamp. We must replace the current ambiguity with a real sense of direction and purpose to ensure that there is a reduction in the number of people abusing drugs in our community. The success of the new policy can be judged by the rise or fall in that statistic.

At the same time, the Scottish Crime and Drug Enforcement Agency must be allowed to stand alone, free from the administrative convenience of a management oversight by the Chief Executive of the Scottish Police Services Authority. After seven years of prevarication, the Sir Humphrey-style decision to avoid institutional conflict by treating the Agency as merely an 'economic unit' within the SPSA is perverse. That decision which was based on no significant business case, ensured the Director General was required to account in budget and other terms to a chief executive, and through him to a board. It is a policy suitable for those committed to a dogma but it is nonetheless completely unsatisfactory and inefficient.

Current members of the Scottish Parliament and the previous Scottish Executive had originally planned to avoid this *Yes Minister* result, by providing the SCDEA with a purpose-made board which would ensure an effective governance and oversight of this essential police work. In the era of counter-terrorism and organised crime threats, the Agency deserves nothing less. There can be no operational independence where critical decisions about people and finance reside outwith the Agency.

On two occasions, the Justice Committee of the Scottish Parliament has recommended that the head of the SCDEA be given the equivalent status of a Chief Constable. The current arrangement ignores that recommendation and leaves the Director General as servant to the Council of

Chief Constables which controls the strategic and financial decisions that affect Scotland's law enforcement community.

It is, however, essential in a democratic society that the Director General is held to account by a board of people who have a clear understanding of the challenges to be faced by operational policing rather than being driven largely by how much everything costs. A well-chosen properly constituted board would really be able to put the Director General's operational decisions under the microscope and know he was doing the right thing for Scotland at all times.

Critical to the SCDEA's success is its ability to act swiftly and decisively to counter the threat from serious organised crime, no matter from where it comes. The Scottish people and the economic stability of our nation depend on serious organised crime being tackled in such a decisive manner. They deserve nothing less.

Given a positive lead from our politicians on these two issues, Scotland requires – and is entitled to – a world-leading Crime Campus to maintain the nation's commitment to tackling serious organised crime. The current five years of delay in delivering this project cannot continue.

Internationally, Scotland is acknowledged as a relatively crime-free environment. We have managed to avoid the worst excesses of corruption and organised criminality evident in other parts of the world. It is essential, for the sake of our children's future, in this increasingly globalised society, that serious organised crime is not tolerated here. Across the world, there are many nations where the leaders now wished they had responded much more quickly to such threats.

Finally, I hope my frank comments throughout this book show that police officers are human beings and as such they are capable of making mistakes often in difficult circumstances. However, we should also remember that police officers also contribute immensely to the well-being of our society, something we are all able to enjoy.

Looking back over this time, I have come to see a career in the police as a worthy and honourable ambition, whether as a constable or a chief. The honour is in doing what is right and giving of your best for others, no matter your rank. That tradition of public service must be maintained. My lasting memories of the decades include the selfless commitment from anonymous police officers and staff, often outwith the gaze of the general public.

I have but two regrets. The first is that I should have taken more time to enjoy the companionship and success I have experienced over the years. Unfortunately, time passed too quickly to allow that. I remember now the many people, outwith the police as well as colleagues, who kept me going over the years. In my twenties, ten years seemed a lifetime but at this stage of my life the thought of ten years ahead seems so brief in the scheme of things.

Secondly, I wish I could have been left to conclude my business at the Scottish Crime and Drug Enforcement Agency. I sincerely hope, however, that those who follow after me are given the opportunity to do what is required and the support they so earnestly deserve. In spite of these regrets, I look back now on my life in the police with pride and satisfaction.

I am also fortunate to be looking forward to a future full of interest and a new-found freedom.